UNDERSTANDING AND LIVING WITH PEOPLE WHO ARE MENTALLY ILL

ABOUT THE AUTHOR

Dr. Soukup is a licensed psychologist and a Nationally Certified Senior Addictions Counselor. He has a B.S. in business, an MBA, an MA in counseling and a Doctor of Psychology degree.

He is on the Adjunctive Faculty of the Adler School of Professional Psychology and serves on the National Board of Trustees of the Forest Institute of Psychology. Dr. Soukup is a member of the American Psychological Association and the Illinois Psychological Association. He is on the Allied Staff of four private psychiatric hospitals in the Chicago area as well as in private practice.

Dr. Soukup specializes in neuropsychology, psychological assessment and clinical treatment. He works with children, adolescents, adults and families in outpatient as well as inpatient settings. As a teacher, therapist and clinician he has extensive knowledge and experience in the diagnosis and treatment of mental illness.

UNDERSTANDING AND LIVING WITH PEOPLE WHO ARE MENTALLY ILL

Techniques to Deal With
Mental Illness in the Family

By

JAMES E. SOUKUP, NCACII, MBA, PSY.D.

CHARLES C THOMAS · PUBLISHER
Springfield · Illinois · U.S.A.

Published and Distributed Throughout the World by

CHARLES C THOMAS • PUBLISHER
2600 South First Street
Springfield, Illinois 62794-9265

© *1995 by* CHARLES C THOMAS • PUBLISHER

ISBN 0-398-05940-3

Library of Congress Catalog Card Number: 94-35453

Printed in the United States of America
SC-R-3

Library of Congress Cataloging-in-Publication Data

Soukup, James E.
    Understanding and living with people who are mentally ill :
techniques to deal with mental illness in the family / by James E.
Soukup.
        p.   cm.
    Includes index.
    ISBN 0-398-05940-3
    1. Mentally ill — Family relationships.   2. Mental illness.
3. Mentally ill — Home care.   4. Adjustment (Psychology)   I. Title.
    [DNLM: 1. Mental Disorders — psychology — popular works.
2. Adaptation, Psychological.   3. Family.   WM 100 S725u   1995]
RC455.4.F3S67   1995
616.89 — dc20
DNLM/DLC
for Library of Congress   94-35453
                                                                CIP

PREFACE

Each year from 16 to 20 million Americans suffer from major depression. Even more individuals are impaired by anxiety disorders. It is estimated that 13 percent of the population abuse or are dependent on alcohol and other mood altering drugs. As our population ages, more and more people suffer from Alzheimer's disease. Over two million Americans are diagnosed as schizophrenic.

At one time or another, it is probable that every family will experience mental illness. Living with mental illness in the family is difficult and often has a negative emotional impact on family members. Common responses are feelings of anxiety, guilt, hopelessness, helplessness, depression, shame, codependence, anger, and confusion.

The purpose of this book is to help family members understand mental illness and develop healthy, functional, and appropriate attitudes and responses. This book will also be of interest to students, counselors, and therapists by assisting them to understand the concerns, emotional responses, and problems facing family members. With this knowledge, the therapist can help the family develop coping plans and techniques.

Symptoms, treatment approaches, and advice on obtaining help are discussed. Disorders described include alcoholism, Alzheimer's disease, mood disorders, sexual and spouse abuse, rage episodes, obsessive compulsive disorders, anxiety disorders, sexual dysfunction, bulimia and anorexia nervosa, adolescent suicide and depression, and attention deficit disorders.

Other subjects included are stress management techniques, codependency, self-help groups, adult children of alcoholics (ACOA) issues, effective parenting techniques, the use of psychotropic drugs in treatment, and various types of psychotherapy.

J.E.S.

CONTENTS

UNDERSTANDING AND LIVING WITH PEOPLE WHO ARE MENTALLY ILL

Section I

Chapter I

THE NATURE, PREVALENCE AND
DIAGNOSIS OF MENTAL DISORDERS

The *Diagnostic and Statistical Manual of Mental Disorders* (*Fourth Edition*) defines a mental disorder as " . . . a clinically significant behavioral or psychological syndrome or pattern that occurs in an individual and is associated with present distress (e.g., a painful symptom) or disablity (i.e., an impairment in one or more important areas of functioning) or with a significant increase of risk of suffering, death, pain, disability or loss of freedom" (p. xxi, introduction). The syndrome must be more than an expected response to an event such as grief with the death of a loved one.

In the case of a mental illness, the disorder creates distress, disability and/or other risks. The distress is more than a passing distress. It must be persistent. (Symptoms less than 6 months are considered acute, over 6 months chronic.) If functional impairment occurs it must be in major life areas such as career, family, social, financial. The "risks" referred to are such things as injuring self or others, inability to care for self, and inability to function independently.

The definition is "wordy" however it is important for a family member to understand the nature as well as characteristics of the particular mental disorder affecting the family. Mental disorders vary in intensity and severity, however in order to fit the diagnostic criteria there must be a significant level of distress and/or dysfunction or risk thereof.

Mental disorders are common in our society. Emotional illness has been recorded since the beginning of history. However, there has been a tendency to consider mental disorders in a negative light. Individuals accept and seek medical treatment for physical disorders. However, many mental disorders go undiagnosed and untreated.

Mental disorders are more prevalent than one might think. According to the American Psychological Association, at any one time, 18 percent of Americans (including 18 million children) suffer from a diagnosable mental disorder. One percent of the population is considered to be schizophrenic. Conservative estimates place the number of people in the U.S. who have a depressive episode at between 10 and 20 million. (Fifty-five percent of the population is diagnosed as having a significant depression at least once in a lifetime.) The prevalence of anxiety disorder is even greater in the U.S. population than depression, although symptoms often are not treated or diagnosed. Personality disorders often create severe career, family and relationship problems, however, like anxiety disorders, often are untreated. Psychoactive substance use disorders (alcohol and other mood altering drug abuse and dependence) tend to destroy families and impair the functional ability of family members in adulthood. A recent study reported that 13 percent of the adult population could be classified as alcohol abusers or dependent on alcohol at some time in their lives. Adolescent depression and suicide as well as gang membership and chemical abuse and dependency are on the rise. With increased longevity there is also an increase in senile dementia (Alzheimers). Very few families are untouched by mental disorder.

Diagnosing the disorder as well as family responses to the individual who is impaired is important in treatment. Care must be taken to distinguish between "emotional problems" and "mental disorders," although the author has used the term "emotional problems" in the text to discuss and describe symptoms. (A sequel to this book is planned to deal with techniques of coping with less severe problems such as divorce adjustment and grief, although many techniques mentioned in this book are appropriate.) The reader must realize that there is a real difference, for example, between people who are depressed and those with major depression. The same applies to individuals who are anxious and tense as opposed to those who suffer from panic disorder. Using alcohol is quite different than abusing alcohol or being chemically dependent with alcohol the drug of choice. The problems related to living with individuals who have a mental disorder are usually severe and disturbing to the family system as well as the individual members of the family. Other situations and conditions can also be disturbing. The *DSM-IV* lists conditions not attributed to a mental disorder that are significant. These include such things as child-parent problems, marital problems and "phase of life circumstances."

Recently a leading weekly magazine published an article entitled, "Crybabies and Tattletales." The article claimed that the 1990's was a time of "crybabies and tattletales" and that there is a tendency in our society to blame others for our faults and problems. The article continued that we, as a society, also have developed a sense of entitlement and that we tend to be jealous and resentful of those who have more than we do. Hopefully, individuals using this book will recognize the possibility of blaming others and using the label "mentally ill." Often comments such as, "The relationship failed because he or she is mentally ill" or has emotional problems, is heard in therapy.

Often individuals who have problems with relationships label the significant other as "alcoholic" or characterologically disturbed. Of course, there are a number of people who are alcoholics or suffer from personality disorders; however our diagnosis must be based on more than a tendency to blame. Blaming the other person relieves us of the necessity of taking the responsibility for our own happiness and our own life.

There is also a tendency to project. Projection is to classify or identify the other individual as possessing feelings or characteristics which we ourselves possess. Individuals who are depressed, for example, often see depression in those around them. In dealing with mental illness in a family we must recognize the possibility of blaming others for our own faults or labeling others falsely.

The diagnosis of mental disorders requires very specialized clinical training. The purpose of this book is to help family members and significant others to develop better methods and techniques in dealing with mental disorders. It is not intended to encourage individuals to diagnose mental illness. The criteria and symptoms listed in this book under each category of disorder are included for educational purposes as is the discussion regarding associated features, course, complications and prevalence of the disorder.

Many individuals who suffer from mental disorders have been diagnosed either as an inpatient in a psychiatric hospital or on an outpatient basis. It is important to be aware of how these diagnoses were made and the qualifications of the diagnostician. The symptoms of schizophrenia and the manic episodes of a bipolar disorder are usually so extreme and often so debilitating that professional help has been sought and a diagnosis provided. Other disorders are not as obvious. Depressive symptoms in the elderly are often classified as Alzheimer's. The symptoms may be due to depression.

Diagnosis may be made by individuals with limited credentials and abilities. Someone once stated, "If the only tool you have is a hammer, everything looks like a nail." There is an alarming trend of untrained individuals making diagnostic judgements. The reader should be aware of this as well as the possibility of blaming interpersonal problems or other problems on the pathology of another.

It is important to emphasize that an accurate and valid diagnosis is primary not only in the treatment of an individual who has emotional problems but also in developing an appropriate and functional way of dealing with the pathology by family members. Although individuals who suffer from mental disorders often resist treatment (and assessment) professional help is often vital.

A diagnosis provides a conceptual framework and reference point. Often family members are confused, angry and overwhelmed, especially if the mental disorder is acute and just developing. Knowing more about the disorder and realizing that help is available is an important first step in developing an adaptive and helpful way of dealing with mental illness in the family.

Chapter II

THE IMPACT OF MENTAL ILLNESS ON THE FAMILY

Shame, Anxiety, Anger, Codependency, and Dysfunction

A family can be considered a system. Each family system differs; however, they all have rules (often unwritten), member roles (roles in the family as well as outside the family), secrets, rituals and relationship patterns.

Mental illness in the family impacts or affects each family differently because of differences in each system. However, generally, emotional illness tends to cause emotional responses from family members. These responses are often responses of anxiety, anger, codependence, shame and dysfunction.

It has been documented that emotional illness in the family causes shame. Alcoholism in a family, for example, is often denied or kept secret because of fear of exposure. Family members often collude to keep mental illness a secret not only from the community but also from relatives and friends. This denial often precludes treatment of the individual's mental and emotional illness. Family members often make excuses for the mentally ill individual in the system. Social engagements are sometimes missed because of such things as a panic attack, an episode of depression, or an alcoholic binge. Family members tend to use denial, minimizing, and rationalization to defend against emotional illness in the family.

Anxiety in the family system results in pathological responses, roles and rules. Particular situations may be avoided. In cases where stress creates the possibility of an episode of depression, anxiety or drinking, the family members make special arrangements or are particularly vigilant and anxious. For example, if the mentally ill family member tends to decompensate (i.e., respond in a pathological manner) when on vacation, the family may attempt to compensate by not taking vacations. Fear of an episode (whether it be depression, abuse of alcohol and other mood altering drugs, a bipolar condition, anxiety or a psychotic breakdown) tends to dictate family plans. Soon the family's social life and the functional abilities of other family members are controlled by the behaviors of the person who is mentally ill.

This syndrome or family system response, of course depends not only on the particular family system but also the nature of the mental illness. One of the variables as far as the disorder is the chronicity of the illness. Many mental illnesses are episodic—where the individual functions fairly adequately between episodes. Schizophrenia, bipolar disorders and major depression are often controlled by psychotherapy and/or medication. However, family members may be exposed to recurrent episodes. In situations where the emotional illness is acute and episodic, there is a tendency for the family system to live in a suspended state of anxiety with the fear that an episode will occur.

Individuals who grow up in alcoholic homes tend to suffer from chronic feelings of anxiety and uncertainty. (More will be written about Adult Children of Alcoholics (ACOA) responses, dealing with ACOA issues and codependency.) The episodes of mental illness create feelings of anxiety and dysphoria. There tends to be generalized feelings of anxiety or fear that an episode will occur. This anxiety is as harmful to family members as are the feelings related to the acute episode itself.

Examples of this might be the family of an individual who is in partial recovery from drug dependency, or the case of an individual who exhibits symptoms of rage. The family lives in fear that an episode will take place. Behaviors of family members are modified in an attempt to prevent the occurrence of an episode. Marriages are often based on accommodation of the mentally ill spouse. Of course, this results in a controlled, unhealthy relationship. Individuals who are abused in a relationship tend to develop a style of accommodation. Anxiety responses in a family system to episodic mental illness is often episodic itself, in nature. In other words, the family member feels a generalized anticipatory level of anxiety with an increase in anxiety occurring during the episode.

Chronic mental illness (defined as a disorder which tends to be continuous and long term) also creates a great deal of anxiety in the family system. However, this anxiety differs from anxiety as a response to episodic mental illnesses. Anxiety in response to a chronic mental illness tends to be more pervasive. The anxiety tends to be more chronic just as the illness is more chronic. Schizophrenia, depression, anxiety disorders and attention deficit disorders tend to be chronic in nature although the functional level varies. These disorders can often be controlled by psychotherapy and/or medication. Personality disorders such as passive aggressive, and antisocial and borderline personality disorder, tend to be characterological and do not respond as readily to medication although medication might treat secondary conditions such as situational depression. (More will be written about specific disorders in the family and how they affect you as an individual.) Chronic mental illness in a family tends to take its toll on the other members. Anxiety, over a period of time, creates particular responses. Often spouses and parents develop a form of depersonalization. They no longer respond emotionally because past experiences have been so difficult and/or painful. Often there are feelings of hopelessness and helplessness. Family members often feel trapped by the individual who is emotionally disturbed and by the individual's illness.

Anger is also a common response with the feelings of, "Why did this have to happen to me." Or, "Why did this have to happen in my family." In many cases, however, this anger is unexpressed. It is often unexpressed because of fear of an episodic response or because expression of anger in the past has not improved conditions. Unresolved anger results in increased tension and anxiety. Following chapters discuss adaptive methods of dealing with anger, anxiety, denial and codependency.

Briefly, codependence is an attempt on the part of one person to provide, completely, for the needs of a second person. Often this takes place in a family system where one member is emotionally ill. The urge to provide for the other person is often done out of love. However, the results are usually disasterous to both parties. No one can completely anticipate the needs of another anymore than they can provide completely for these needs. This results in failure. The dependent person becomes resentful. The codependent becomes unappreciated. No one's needs are met. The emotional illness in the family system tends to increase without treatment or improvement.

Dysfunction is common in a family with mental illness. This is in part related to the fact that we treat symptoms and not the impact of the disorder on the family. As a society we expect immediate "cure" for emotional problems. Medication is sometimes prescribed without consideration of the causal factors and the impact which the emotional problems have had not only on the individual himself but also on the family. In situations where the emotional illness may be alleviated by medication there are often the residual family dysfunctional roles, rules and behaviors.

Roles often have become unhealthy and dysfunctional. The parent may become overly responsible and protective of the child. The child might become the responsible parent. Parental and generational boundaries often become blurred. In the case of marital conflict caused by mental illness, parents often turn to one of the children for love, attention and satisfaction. Rituals are developed to hide the shame of mental illness. Relationships are often based on anxiety and anger. Needs are not met, because individuals tend to focus on the needs/demands of the family member who is depressed, anxious, inadequate or dysfunctional. Sense of self is poorly developed because of a preoccupation with the individual who has emotional problems.

Family systems differ in the ability to deal with stress such as emotional illness, just as individuals differ. Individual abilities are related to environmental and conditioning factors as well as dispositional and genetic factors. Some people are more able to handle stress. Others tend to develop somatic and/or emotional problems themselves, especially when exposed to prolonged stress.

Individuals develop different defenses to deal with stressors. Psychology discusses "ego defenses" and how we use them to defend against psychological injury. We have mentioned some of these defenses. Defenses, including denial, minimizing, rationalizing, depersonalization and withdrawal are common. It should be remembered that these defenses are not always detrimental to the individual in a stress situation such as dealing with a member in the family with episodic or chronic mental illness. Often ego defenses are utilized to allow the family member to prepare a more appropriate, adequate "defense" or way of dealing with the episode or situation. (Psychology calls the adaptive use of ego defenses "Active Regression in Service of Ego"—ARISE.) Hopefully this book will help you distinguish between healthy and unhealthy ways of dealing with mental illness in the family.

Dispositional and characterological factors also differentiate individuals and their ability to deal with family members who have mental problems. Some individuals are insecure and tend to be vulnerable to the opinions of society. Many situations of mental disorder have been hidden because of fear of outside knowledge of the problems. Individuals who tend to be anxious or depressed are often more severely impacted by mental illness in the family. (As was discussed, anxiety and depression are often secondary responses among family members.) Individuals without a strong support system tend to have greater problems with stress. Those who have problems trusting others and disclosing their feelings tend to resist asking for help for themselves. (Often in families with a mentally ill member, the patient is identified as the only one "needing help." This is not true.) Individuals with a strong sense of identity, who have defined their needs, interests and goals tend to separate more adequately and are more able to handle stress in the family.

The individual's ability to deal with mental illness in the family also tends to be related to past experiences. Mental disabilities similar to those experienced in family of origin often create increased anxiety. An individual married to someone who is chronically depressed tends to reexperience childhood memories related, for example, to a depressed parent. Fear of abuse is common among those who have witnessed abuse in the family of origin. An alcoholic spouse triggers childhood responses to an alcoholic parent. An individual who has gone through an abusive or dysfunctional marriage tends to respond with anxiety and tension when similar situations appear to be developing in current relationships.

A final consideration in the discussion of the impact of mental illness on the family is related to the extended family. Individuals in the immediate family are usually more severely impacted. The primary caretaker (whether it be the spouse of an alcoholic, the parent of a child with attention deficit disorder or the adult child of an individual with Alzheimer's disease) is, of course, involved on a day-to-day basis. However, members of the extended family are impacted.

More distant relatives are often consulted and confided in by the immediate family members. In-laws, uncles, aunts and cousins often become confidants. Commonly, in a divorce, family members are called on to "take sides." In cases of mental illness extended family members are often asked to give advice or help with the care taking responsibilities. Advice given by relatives is not always practical or therapeutic. This must be remembered. However, extended family can be utilized in the development of a support system. Often extended family can give the principle caretaker "a break" from responsibilities (more will be said about developing a stress management plan and outside interests). Sharing feelings with extended family also tends to be helpful.

Day-to-day involvement and involvement in treatment by extended members will depend on relationships which have developed over time, and the dynamics of the particular family. My experience has been that grandparents often are very significant in their relationship to children and adolescents in a family. (One of the most significant and often repeated "losses" identified by children and adolescents during a clinical interview is the death of a grandparent. Incidently, one of the most pleasurable is usually a family trip or vacation.)

The decision to inform extended family members of mental health problems is an individual one. The "need to know" and the "right to know" varies. However, it must be realized that mental illness in one family often impacts other family systems.

This book is an attempt to help you develop specific techniques to deal with your own situation based on the type disorder, your individual response style, strengths and weaknesses; dynamics within the family; and other particulars such as the nature of the extended family.

Chapter III

SPECIFIC TECHNIQUES FOR DEALING
WITH MENTAL DISORDER IN THE FAMILY

Living in a family where one or more members suffers from a mental disorder creates stress just as other situations such as medical illness, divorce or death of a loved one results in stress. The members of the family system are affected. The degree of stress depends on a number of factors. These include the severity of the disorder; whether the disorder is chronic or acute (and the duration of the episode if the disorder is acute); the relationship of the impaired family member to the individual members; and the nature of the disorder. The ability to cope with mental illness in the family also varies depending on such factors as the ego strength of the family member; support systems available to the family; family experiences with other stressors and family cohesiveness. Stress does not necessarily result in dysfunction. As one writer said, of negative life experiences, "If it doesn't kill you it strengthens you." Of course, this is difficult to accept, as a family member who is experiencing severe stress as the result of mental illness in the family.

This chapter's purpose is to help you, as the affected family member, deal with the negative impact and stress created by living in a family with mental disorder. Specific suggestions will be given which apply to many categories of disorder. Later in the book particular disorders will be discussed to give you a better understanding of the nature, course and treatment of each, as well as additional strategies for dealing with each type of mental illness. Many of the suggestions provided below also apply to dealing with stress in other life situations such as marital conflict, job problems and interpersonal relationships. The techniques suggested give you, the reader, a number of clinically sound and proven techniques to maintain your own sense of self, your own mental health and a perspective in life which is positive and adaptive. How you use these techniques depends not only on your own personality, and emotional make up, but also on the particular family system and your life situation.

Your relationship to the family member, of course, affects your choice of responses. A parent-child relationship is quite different than a marital situation where one person is mentally ill. Your value system, upbringing, and priorities also affect your choices. Religious views and beliefs may limit you as far as considering divorce as an option. Many religions and individuals believe that the vows "in sickness and in health" apply to mental illness as well as physical illness. Certainly, leaving or even confronting an abusive alcoholic spouse is difficult if your value system precludes such a move.

Choice of techniques is also dependent on personality style and traits. Over the years each of us has developed a way of dealing with adversity, crisis and trauma. Some individuals are passive and reactive. Others have few problems setting boundaries and limits. You, as the reader, will have to decide which techniques are most comfortable. Many of the techniques such as developing a stress management plan are applicable in other situations and probably desirable for most people. However, individuals who are shy, dependent and avoidant might have problems developing social interests and becoming involved in social activities outside the family.

Approach the techniques discussed open mindedly. Realize that changing the way you respond to a situation changes the dynamics. There are options in life. Too often we become rigid and limit our choices. Consider your needs, your self-interest and your own health. If you do this, these techniques will help you develop a plan which is beneficial not only to you but to the individual who is mentally ill as well as other members in the family.

1. The first technique in dealing with mental disorder in the family is to become completely educated as to the nature, course, treatment and prognosis of the disorder. This advice, of learning all one can of a situation that is stressful, applies to many cases of crisis, trauma and possible danger. When one is threatened with unemployment or the possibility of a divorce it is wise to consider the facts and possibilities for the future. Education allows one to make more accurate and adequate choices and decisions.

Often mental illness develops over a period of time and the individual tends to ignore the impact on their own stability and sanity. Such is the case, usually with alcoholism and, often, physical abuse. It is important to recognize the symptoms of a mental disorder as early as possible in order to plan adaptive strategies and to develop a method of dealing with the situation as soon as possible. Hopefully the second part of this book will help you to at least be aware of various mental disorders.

Denial also tends to impair knowledge and action. It is important that you evaluate accurately the interactions within your family system or in your relationship with significant others if you, yourself, are feeling dysphoric, abused, unhappy or unfulfilled. The problems may be related to poor communication, failure to identify needs, lack of assertiveness or to more serious problems such as major depression, alcoholism or bipolar disorder.

2. The second suggestion is to seek expert advice and help. Common reactions to mental disorder in the family are confusion, fear, anxiety, anger and often guilt. In the situation of the initial episode of an acute mental disorder, family members are often overwhelmed. The cause of the disruptive and/or dysfunctional behavior is unknown. The family searches for answers. Answers are available through individuals who are trained to diagnose and treat mental illness.

Often the individual suffering from the disorder resists contact with a professional just like many (including myself) resist medical and dental evaluations. The thought of mental illness is often terrifying. Confronting the individual in a positive, nonemotional way is a technique in encouraging a diagnosis and/or treatment. The most effective way of doing this is to focus on the symptoms and the behaviors. Too often emotions become involved, with one party blaming the other. Helping the individual improve reality testing is one way of helping solve the problem. Demanding a change in behavior or attitude is not. As was discussed, telling someone who is depressed to be happy is not only foolish, it is insulting.

Those who treat chemical dependence have developed a technique called "intervention." This technique is used to help the individual who is dependent realize the impact of his dependency on the lives of others. Usually a therapist will meet two or three times with family members and allow each individual to identify the impact of the chemical dependent relationships and behaviors on them personally. The therapist and family members then meet with the individual and confront him or her on the negative impact on their lives and feelings. Often this improves reality testing, overcomes denial, and allows for the development of a treatment plan. Intervention strategies can be used in other situations such as with an adolescent who is acting out in an antisocial way.

Obtaining professional help and advice can also be facilitated by other individuals who are significant to the family member who is having problems. Ministers and physicians can provide improved reality testing and recommend professional help.

If the individual does not seek help, family members should not hesitate to see a professional alone. In fact, individual therapy is often a valuable technique in dealing with one's own feelings regarding the mental illness of a family member. As was discussed, mental illness is a family disease. Members of the family often develop symptoms such as depression, anxiety or depersonalization. Responses to the person with the disorder often, over time, are unhealthy. In some cases they exacerbate the problems in the family. These unhealthy symptoms and response should be addressed.

3. A third recommendation is involvement in treatment. There is a tendency to identify the individual with a mental illness as the "patient." (In many cases the identified patient is not the primary cause of the dysfunction in a family. During divorce or in the situation of marital conflict, it is not uncommon for adolescents and/or children to act out. This is a call for help.) Often mental health professionals are called on to "fix the patient." As a society we appear to want an immediate cure for our problems. The cure is considered "better" if it involves someone else changing their behaviors and attitudes rather than our making changes. There is a tendency to condemn the individual who displays symptoms of mental disorder and blame them for all of the interpersonal problems we are experiencing. Divorce rationalizations often include, "He was an alcoholic," "She was always depressed," "I couldn't stand her mood swings." This may be true; however helping an individual with mental illness and reacting in a healthy, adaptive way requires that we separate the behavior from the individual and support the individual in a nonjudgemental positive way. Involvement in treatment will not only improve understanding but help you, as a family member, to make adaptive changes in your interactions and in the relationship.

4. Consider joining a support group. We are in a age, hopefully, of mutual support and understanding. There are, of course, treatment support groups such as Overeaters Anonymous (OA), Cocaine Anonymous (CA) and Alcoholics Anonymous (AA). There are also support groups for family members. The most commonly known groups are

related to chemical dependence and include Alanon, Alateen and Adult Children of Alcoholics (ACOA). There are also codependency groups as well as groups for parents of mentally ill adolescents and parents and family members of individuals who are schizophrenic. Parents and family members have also formed groups to deal with bipolar disorders in the family and teenage suicide as well as unresolved grief and loss of loved ones. Psychiatric hospitals as well as community mental health facilities often offer leadership for such groups.

The advantage of joining a group is to share feelings and ventilate repressed emotions. It is easier to talk about negative experiences with those who have had similar experiences. Groups also provide support, relieve feelings of guilt, and allow for the sharing of coping techniques.

Chapter IV

SPECIFIC COPING TECHNIQUES CONTINUED

5. Become aware of the behaviors in your family due to mental illness, your feelings and your responses. Emotional awareness is important in changing attitudes and behaviors. As an individual you respond in a very unique and special way to the stress and situations that arise from mental illness. Being aware of your feelings and how you respond will not only help you develop more adaptive responses but also feelings of being in control of your life and life situation. One very common characteristic of those dealing with family members with mental disorders is a sense of powerlessness. Individuals in a family tend to react rather than be proactive. The non-abusing spouse, for example, in an alcoholic family tends to attempt to read the attitudes and feelings of the chemical dependent individual and respond in ways that will not cause problems. The alcoholic rules by creating an atmosphere of anxiety and fear. Thus, the spouse defocuses from the real problem and attempts to provide a stressfree environment. Of course, for the spouse (or in some cases other family members) the environment is anything but stress-free. The enabler is always on the alert. Always vigilant. Always tense.

The same response is often common with individuals who suffer from bipolar disorder, rage episodes, and depression. Significant others tend to live a life of anxiety and fear, wondering when the next episode will take place.

Keeping a journal as to incidents which cause you stress, your emotional state related to these incidents and your response will help you identify unhealthy patterns of response as well as help you develop better ways of coping with stressful incidents. If an individual's depression causes you to become angry and lash out, it is time to develop a new way of dealing with the episode.

6. One response, and the sixth technique of dealing with mental illness, is creative detachment. Families, with one member who suffers from mental illness, often become emeshed. Sometimes there is even a shared psychopathology or a Folie à deaux where a healthy family mem-

ber develops symptoms similar to the mentally ill individual. It is difficult to separate because of codependency and dependency. However, separation and detachment is necessary to gain a realistic perspective on the illness and the individual's problems. This is difficult because individuals in a significant relationship have established a pattern of action—reaction. One way to detach is to withhold your response. Interpersonal problems related to mental illness often become shouting matches or power struggles. It is best not to respond when feeling overwhelmed or angry. Time allows us to more accurately consider the situation and not be negatively affected by the behaviors of others.

7. Involvement in activities away from the home and the development of other interests is an important way of relieving stress and focusing on self. This is important. Many individuals involved in a relationship with someone who is mentally ill report they have "lost" their identity. The individual with the mental illness and the related secondary problems tend to take precedent. Individuals lose sight of their own goals and needs. Life revolves around the member with the emotional problems. This same pattern also develops in relationships where one of the members is severely ill physically.

An exercise that might be of benefit is to list on a piece of paper five goals for the week. These should be goals which are enjoyable and have been postponed because of stress or preoccupation with another's problems. Focus on accomplishing these goals during the week (they can be minor such as going to a movie alone or cleaning out a closet). Another exercise is to list five emotional needs. Everyone has different needs. Some people have a need for acceptance. Others, to provide and care for. Still others, to be cared for by someone else. Some people place influence and power in a position of predominance. Others have a need to be accepted and loved. List your needs and then rate how well they are satisfied. It is common for people in dysfunctional families to have a very low level of need satisfaction.

Finally, list five things that you like about yourself and five things which you would like to change. Place time limits on when you are going to make changes.

These suggestions are all related to reclaiming yourself as a valuable unique, special person and to helping you to live a life outside of and in addition to what might be going on around you in the family or in a significant relationship. Finding new interests, becoming involved in outside activities, setting goals, focusing on fun and personal happiness and beginning to get in touch with self are all important ways of dealing with the stress, concern, anxiety and dysphoria in a family situation that tends to create unhealthy responses, attitudes and feelings.

8. Rid yourself of guilt. Individuals tend to internalize a sense of responsibility for mental illness in the family. Much has been written about the schizophrenic family with the dominant mother and the unavailable submissive father. (Research has proven that this dynamic is fictional.) Spouses of chemical dependent individuals tend to feel responsible. Parents of children who suffer from attention deficit hyperactivity disorder often believe that the disorder is genetic and their fault. Because there appears to be a predisposition for schizophrenia, depression, and bipolar disorder in families, it is not uncommon for parents to blame themselves (or their spouse).

There is a great deal of research to be done on the causal factors of mental disorders. Feeling guilty does not solve problems. Helping the significant other or family member with a mental disorder is much more therapeutic. Trying to understand the disorder and providing support is a better response than feeling guilty. Do not condemn the family member with the disorder. Do not condemn yourself.

9. Developing a stress management plan is important not only in dealing with mental illness in the family but also in life. Much has been written about the benefits as well as procedures. Developing a program of exercise, proper diet and relaxation are the three important factors in a stress management plan. Individuals under stress often have problems following through on a plan. This is unfortunate. Dealing with stress becomes much easier and a pattern when involved in a workable plan.

Chapter V

MORE TECHNIQUES

10. Changing unhealthy rules, roles and rituals in a family system is another technique in dealing with mental illness. Much has been written about chemically dependent families and unhealthy roles, rules and rituals in these families. These families are often referred to as "dysfunctional families." Some of the same principles apply to families where one member is suffering from a severe mental disorder. Unhealthy roles in a family tend to exacerbate problems and functional disability not only of the impaired member but of other members in the family.

One of the roles is that of "an enabler." An enabler is one who perpetuates problems by denying their existence or performing tasks for the individual who is ill, rather than encouraging the person to take responsibility. In the case of an adolescent drug abuser, the parent might act in ways which lessen the consequences of negative and/or antisocial behaviors. The parents may lie to school, cover for absence from work, or defend the adolescent in court when legal problems develop. Enablers in an alcoholic family tend to minimize, protect, rescue and "cover up" for the individual who is chemically dependent. Family system analysts refer to the "chief enabler," who is super responsible and tends to be a martyr. This individual is the family caretaker. He or she takes control of the family and is most dependent on the individual with problems. Externally the individual presents as caring and understanding. Internally the person feels anger, anxiety and inadequacy.

Another role is that of "family hero." This individual is the visible success in the family. For example, in a family where one of the parents is severely disabled by recurrent episodes of depression, the hero defocuses by becoming a success in areas visual to community such as sports or academic achievement. This person represents family feelings of pride and self-worth. In reality, the individual is usually anxious, and unsure. Rather than dealing with family problems related to mental illness, the hero usually leaves the family system early. This "escape" or flight often results in problems later on in life.

Another role is that of "scapegoat." The scapegoat is the center of negative attention and takes the focus off problems in a dysfunctional family. This individual often acts in antisocial ways. Internal feelings of hurt, loneliness, anger and fear are often covered by a rigid wall of defenses.

A fourth role, which is often found in a family suffering from mental illness (as well as the alcoholic family), is that of "lost or forgotten child." This is the individual who tends to be withdrawn and lonely. This individual learns not to make close connections in the family. As adults they often are isolated and depressed.

A fifth role is that of "mascot." This individual defocuses from family problems by providing comic relief. Internally the person is fragile, immature and despondent.

As was discussed, these roles initially were identified as unhealthy roles taken by members of families in which one or more members are chemically dependent; however it is possible for these roles to develop in other types of families such as those where a member is mentally ill.

Rules and rituals which are unhealthy also often develop in a family system. Again these are often based on denial and failure to face the reality of mental illness in the family. Symptoms and problems related to the mental illness may be overlooked or minimized. Children may not be allowed to discuss a parent's problem. Individuals who suffer from anxiety, for example, may be unable to participate in social activities or perform work functions. Rather than seek treatment, the family might make arrangements to allow the individual to stay home. The family, as the result of the impaired family member, might become isolated and limited in social contact. Family members may cancel holiday celebrations because of the depression of one member. Rituals and rules which perpetuate illness must be identified and changed.

11. Testing reality. Individuals who are mentally ill often have their own sense of reality and often this sense is distorted. Schizophrenics suffer from delusions and other forms of psychosis causing them to be confused. Their responses and behaviors are often irrational, chaotic and sometimes violent. Individuals who abuse a spouse rationalize that their abuse is appropriate. Active alcoholics deny any negative impact on those around them. Individuals in a manic episode are often disruptive, destructive and present a danger to themselves and others. Depressed individuals tend to focus on their own problems, ignoring the effect of their depression on family members and significant others. It is impor-

tant that you have an accurate impression of reality in dealing with those who are mentally ill.

In determining what reality actually is, it is important to make sure that your views are not distorted. Individuals who have lived with mental illness often develop their own unrealistic patterns of behaviors and attitudes. Make sure that your judgements are not projections. In other words, make sure that your emotions are not seen in the behaviors and attitudes of the other individual. If you are depressed or angry or anxious or negative, these emotions may be attributed to the other person. Unresolved issues from the past may also distort your reality.

Individuals who grow up in an alcoholic (chemically dependent) family tend to have a number of distortions from which they operate. (The same is true of individuals from other types of dysfunctional families.) One of the traits common among adult children of alcoholics (ACOA) is distrust because of unkept promises of an alcoholic parent. Another is a sense of confusion in emotions from childhood experiences of love one moment and rejection the next. ACOA's often feel insecure because of financial problems, conflict, threats of divorce and torn love between two parents. Never knowing what will happen at home from one day to the next creates fear and anxiety. Feelings of emptiness, anger and resentment may result from growing up too fast and missing the expected joys and pleasures of childhood. Having too much responsibility as a child can result in the need to control, rigidity and obsessive compulsive traits. Individuals who grow up in an alcoholic family often have problems with emotional awareness and disclosure because they have been forced to hide their feelings during childhood. Often the sober parent cautions the child to "be good or be quiet" for fear that acting out (or expressing normal feelings) will affect the chemically dependent parent. These attitudes and behaviors from family of origin experiences can lead to distortion in our own reality and impair the way we deal with those who are suffering from emotional problems in our present situation or family.

Our own personalities and characterological traits can also impair reality as well as the way we respond to others in the family system. Each of us has our own style. We may tend to be passive, aggressive, over reactive, be obsessive, compulsive, or narcissistic. These personality disorder traits color our images and affect our interactions.

Consider the way you may distort reality in order to more accurately view the situation in your family.

12. We have discussed to some extent common feelings of anger and anxiety in situations where one member is suffering from mental illness. Another emotion which is often experienced by family members, but is overlooked, is that of grief. There is often a sense of loss. Individuals often feel that they have been cheated, that they have lost opportunities, and that experiences in the family have not been rich and fulfilling. They often feel that their needs have not been met.

Children with a sibling who is mentally ill commonly feel that the sibling has been the focus of attention. This is very common in a situation where one of the children has Attention Deficit Hyperactivity Disorder. Siblings often experience the loss of parental attention and availability. Children who grow up in alcoholic homes experience the loss of a "perfect" or happy childhood. When one parent is depressed, the focus of attention commonly is on his or her problems. Psychiatric hospitalization adds to the stress in the family although this intervention may be necessary.

Coping with these feelings of loss and resentment is necessary. This is more than an option. Professional help might be expedient in resolving these feelings of loss and the related grief.

13. Another technique in dealing with mental illness or emotional problems in the family is to open up communication. Family crisis (and often there is crisis in a family suffering from mental illness) is best handled as a family problem. Usually all of the members are affected in some way. Allowing the individuals to discuss and share feelings is an important way of ventilating emotions and dealing with problems in a direct way. Failure to do this is often related to fears that the impact on the person who is having emotional problems will be negative. This fear perpetuates secrets and encourages repressions. Repressed feelings impair individual progress and adult happiness. A parent who is depressed knows this. They feel the despair, hopelessness and helplessness. Family unity and understanding are important in providing support as well as relieving the sufferer of guilt. It is often said that in an alcoholic family there is an elephant in the room but no one will acknowledge the fact. In the fable about the emperor with no clothes the subjects were afraid to reveal the truth. While many individuals tend to be in denial about their emotional problems, hiding the truth is not of benefit. The best time to have a family conference is after the impaired individual accepts his or her condition. However, sometimes denial is never overcome. In such a

case the family members might want to discuss their feelings and experience, as a family, with the help of a trained therapist.

14. Be supportive. This has been discussed previously; however it is so important that it must be reiterated. No one chooses mental illness (although there may be secondary gains from mental illness in some cases). Realize that the individual who is suffering is suffering. Do not become a codependent but try to be loving, understanding and supportive.

15. Another technique is to do all you can and then have faith. Many of the motto's of twelve step programs make sense such as "One Day At A Time," "Let Go, Let God," and "Easy Does It."

16. Another option is to leave. This sounds radical and often is or can be. This is why I have listed this option last. Great gains have been made in the treatment of mental illness in the last years. The majority of individuals who suffer from anxiety, depression, bipolar disorder and even schizophrenia can lead rich, full happy lives. However, other cases and situations are more difficult to treat. Alcoholism has a high rate of recidivism. Personality disorders are difficult to change. Sexual disorders and rage episodes are hard to treat.

In some situations treatment and adjustment within the family can result in good relationships and mental health. In other situations where the individual suffering from mental illness refuses to get help or response to treatment is minimal, dysfunction continues. The family member or significant other may choose to live in such an environment. Change is often frightening and difficult. This is especially true when one has become dependent or a codependent.

In other situations, leaving is not possible or practical such as in the case of an adolescent in a family where a parent is suffering from a severe mental disorder. Sometimes moral values lead to the decision to stay.

As has been discussed, many families with one member who is mentally ill are dysfunctional, and dysfunctional families are difficult to leave. Often there is a sense of obligation. Also, leaving requires developing new roles, rules and rituals. Dysfunctional families create patterns of interaction and behavior which may be chaotic, irrational and pathological; however, these patterns are consistent.

Staying in a dysfunctional relationship or situation, however, leads to personal psychological damage and harm. One's own growth, enrichment and happiness are impeded.

At least, leaving is an option. A successful business executive carried a note in his wallet. He had written this note to himself, following graduation from college. The note said, "To hell with you. I didn't want this job anyway." He was never fired. He kept open the option of leaving if things became too difficult. You have a right to happiness. Keep your options open.

Section II
SPECIFIC MENTAL DISORDERS
AND COPING TECHNIQUES
FOR FAMILY MEMBERS

The following chapters are to help you identify specific symptoms of the most prevalent mental disorders, help you understand the nature of these disorders and help you utilize the specific techniques in dealing with these disorders in your family system. This is not a guide for the diagnosis of various disorders. Once you have identified symptoms it is important to seek professional help. However, you and only you, can understand your own feelings and how mental illness impacts on your own well being and happiness. Utilization of the presented techniques to ease your pain and help you direct your life in a positive and mutually beneficial way will require patience, effort and possibly professional help. However, the initial decision to make changes is in and of itself positive and healthy.

The discussion of various mental illnesses is based on *The Diagnostic and Statistical Manual of Mental Disorders (Fourth Edition)* published by the American Psychiatric Association, Washington, D.C., 1994.

Chapter VI

ANXIETY DISORDERS

Simple Phobia, Social Phobia, Generalized Anxiety, Post-Traumatic Stress, Panic Disorder, Obsessive Compulsive Disorder

D *SM IV* discusses anxiety disorders of childhood or adolescence and anxiety disorders of adulthood (normally considered 18 or over). Childhood and adolescent anxiety disorders include separation anxiety, avoidant disorder and overanxious disorder. This discussion will focus primarily on adult anxiety disorders. Seven percent of the population is judged to suffer from anxiety disorders of varying degrees of severity. The primary features of an anxiety disorder are symptoms of anxiety and avoidant behaviors. Anxiety symptoms include shortness of breath, dizziness, heart palpitations or accelerated rate (tachycardia), trembling, sweating, choking, nausea, numbness, hot or cold flashes, chest pains, fear of dying and or fear of going crazy or doing something uncontrolled. Four of the above mentioned symptoms must be present during an attack for the diagnosis of panic disorder.

Avoidance behaviors include restriction of travel, leaving home or attending social events, requiring a companion to accompany the individual when away from home, avoidance of crowds, standing in line, being in an enclosed place or vehicle; and preoccupation with escape routes.

Anxiety disorders are the most common mental illness in our society, even more prevalent than major depression. Specific phobias are the most common disorder in the general population. A phobia is a persistent, marked and unreasonable fear of a specific object or situation. Exposure to the object or situation almost always provokes an immediate anxiety response. The object or situation is either avoided or endured with intense anxiety. The fear or avoidant behavior must significantly interfere with the person's normal routine, social activities or relationships.

And finally, although the person recognizes that the fear is unreasonable, the anxiety continues.

Elaborate ways are often developed to avoid the anxiety provoking object or situation (stimulus). Often anticipatory anxiety develops which is a fear of the anxiety developing. The individual often becomes vigilant and overly alert to situations, relationships and his or her environment. The most common objects of anxiety involve animals, blood, injury, closed spaces, heights and air travel.

Age of onset varies with animal phobias usually developing in childhood. Fears of heights, driving, closed spaces and air travel begin in the 20's or 30's usually. Females are more likely to develop simple phobias than males. Level of impairment varies, however people with single phobias usually attempt to adjust or compensate for the disorder. Use (and sometimes abuse) of antianxiety medication is common. (Many antianxiety medications are habit forming and addictive.) However, other forms of treatment are resisted. This is unfortunate because a combination of medication and psychotherapy has proven to be very effective in treating anxiety. New techniques have developed in recent years. Without treatment the disorder usually does not remit.

Social phobia is also a very common anxiety disorder. The criteria is a persistent fear of situations where the sufferer fears scrutiny by others and believes that they will respond in an embarrassing way or be humiliated. There is usually anticipatory anxiety. Onset is late childhood or early adolescence. The anxiety is usually persistent and can increase radically with exposure to the feared situation. Social phobia often involves fear of public speaking and generalized fear in other social situations. Social phobia is more common with males than females. Impairment in the case of social phobia is usually not incapacitating.

Generalized anxiety disorder is defined as excessive anxiety and worry about a number of events or activities in one's life. This anxiety must be frequent and have lasted at least six months. Symptoms such as motor tension (restlessness and agitation), autonomic hyperactivity (palpitations, sweating, cold clammy hands) and vigilance (feeling keyed up and irritable or having sleep problems) and fatigue are persistent. An associated feature is commonly mild depression. Age at onset is usually in the 20's and 30's. The depression may follow an episode of major depression. The disorder is equally common in males and females.

Impairment from specific phobia, social phobia and generalized panic disorder is normally mild to moderate. The individual often attempts to compensate. Impact on the family is not as severe as other forms of mental disorders although avoidant behaviors may inconvenience other family members. For example, the spouse might feel limited and restricted in attending social events. Resentment and anger might develop. Children often tend to be embarrassed and make up stories to explain the absence of a parent at a school or social event.

Coping mechanisms include understanding the disorder and encouraging the sufferer in getting treatment. Discussion with children in the case of a parent suffering from an anxiety disorder can often help the child or adolescent become more understanding. Enabling behaviors should be avoided.

The other types of anxiety disorder tend to be more disruptive of family systems and more difficult to deal with because there is often a related element of disability. Post traumatic stress disorder can result in either mild or severe impairment. Post Traumatic Disorder is defined as the development of symptoms including reexperiencing a traumatic event, avoidance of situations and objects associated with the trauma and symptoms of arousal (such as outbursts of anger, sleep disturbance and hypervigilance.) The person must have experienced or witnessed an event that involved actual or threatened death or actual or threat of serious injury with a response of intense fear, helplessness or terror. Mental health professionals are aware of PTS related to the Vietnam War. Now they are beginning to be more aware of PTS related to childhood abuse (especially sexual abuse).

Emotional lability, depression and guilt (often associated with PTSD) may result in suicidal ideations and/or specific self-defeating, counterproductive attitudes and behaviors. Abuse and dependency on alcohol and other mood altering drugs is a common complication. Problems in holding a job and in developing healthy interpersonal relationships can also be related symptoms.

DSM IV also lists an acute stress disorder similar to PTS. However, the disturbance in mood lasts less than four weeks.

Panic disorders are another form of anxiety and are characterized by the presence of unexplained panic attacks. (A sudden and rapid onset of terror and physical symptoms such as chest pain, hyperventilation and sweating.) Panic disorder with and without agoraphobia (fear of leaving home) can be very disruptive, depending on the ways the individual attempts to avoid the attacks. Avoidance which does not impair normal work and living style will usually not impair family functions and family functioning. Severe avoidance often involves the individual being completely house bound. The severity of the attacks also affects the impact on the family. Panic disorders can go into partial and total remission.

Panic disorder is common. Complications include substance abuse (in an attempt to self-medicate) and depression. Average age of onset is the late 20's. Panic with agoraphobia is the most debilitating of the two forms of panic. Agoraphobia, which is the fear of being in places where escape might be difficult or help unavailable, is often restrictive of social, career and family life. In such situations, family members may have to develop their own interests, activities and ways of staying socially involved. This should be discussed with the member with the disability so that he or she does not feel rejected or abandoned. Again, the encouragement of treatment is recommended.

Another type of anxiety disorder is obsessive compulsive disorder which will be discussed in a following chapter.

Chapter VII

ALCOHOL ABUSE AND DEPENDENCE—
FACTS AND FIGURES

Recent reports indicate that from 15 to 18 million Americans are dependent on alcohol, 21 million have smoked cannabis, 3 million have used cocaine and 500,000 people are addicted to cocaine. Drug education efforts have not been significantly effective in decreasing abuse. While teenagers appear to have developed some degree of skepticism regarding cocaine use, abuse of alcohol, hallucinogens and inhalants has increased. Gang control and distribution of drugs is reported as well as an increase in the availability of a more dangerous and addictive form of cocaine called "crack."

It has been estimated that 80 percent of the population is significantly impacted by alcoholism in some way at some time. This impact can be the result of growing up in an alcoholic family. It can be related to living with or having a relationship with someone who abuses alcohol or is chemically dependent. Or it can be related to one's personal abuse of alcohol or dependency. Many of the concepts presented here will apply to abuse and dependency on other forms of mood altering drugs including cocaine, cannabis, hallucinogens and opioids.

First we will discuss the symptoms of abuse and dependence and the prevalence. We will then discuss recent research and findings concerning the impact of alcoholism on individuals growing up in a dysfunctional family as well as specific ways of dealing with negative attitudes and behaviors developed during childhood years. We then move on to problems of living with an alcoholic. Codependence and enabling behavior will be discussed. Treatment of alcoholism and dependence on other mood altering drugs will be discussed. Finally, we will explore specific techniques which you can use in dealing with alcoholism in the family.

Alcohol abuse and dependence is included in *DSM IV* under Substance Use Disorders. Other use disorders include amphetamines, cannabis, cocaine, hallucinogens, inhalants, nicotine, opioids, phencyclidine (PCP), and sedative, hypnotic and anxiolytic drugs. The manual also lists Substance Induced Disorders related to use of these drugs. These disorders include delirium dementia amnestic psychotic disorder and mood and anxiety disorder. In this chapter we shall discuss Substance Use Disorders.

There are many substances used by the general public which alter mood and behavior. Use of such substances is often considered normal and appropriate. Morning coffee is a stimulant as are other forms of caffeine. Recreational use of alcohol is considered as appropriate by some members of society. Many people use sedatives for sleep problems. Antianxiety and antidepressant medication is used to control mood under medical supervision. Psychosis is treated with major tranquilizers. Psychoactive Substance Use Disorders, however, refer to maladaptive behaviors associated with use of substances leading to significant impairment or distress. The symptoms of dependence are the same for all categories of the drugs listed in *DSM IV* although some of the symptoms are more pronounced than others in each category.

Symptoms of dependence include:

1) Use in larger amounts or over a longer period than intended.
2) A desire or one or more unsuccessful attempts to control use.
3) A disproportionate time devoted to procuring the substance, using the substance or recovering from the effects of use.
4) Frequent intoxication or withdrawal symptoms with resulting impairment in functioning at work, school or home or resulting in hazardous behaviors such as driving under the influence of alcohol.
5) Reduction in or withdrawal from important social, occupational or recreational activities.
7) Continued use despite increased social, psychological and physical problems.
7) The development of tolerance where an increasing amount of the drug is needed to get the same effect or the effect decreased with continued use of the same amount of drug. (Alcohol is a drug.)
8) Withdrawal when the person stops or reduces intake of the substance.
9) Use of the substance to relieve or avoid withdrawal symptoms.

The severity of dependence differs. (Many individuals in the treatment community suggest that the disorder is progressive.) The degrees of severity of dependence include mild where few of the symptoms are present; moderate; and severe with the symptoms significantly impairing functioning. Dependence may be in partial remission (during the past six months some use) or in full remission (no use or evidence of symptoms for six months.) Some treatment specialists state that there is no cure for alcoholism and that abstinence is the only way to eliminate disabling symptoms. They refer to an "active alcoholic" as opposed to one "in recovery."

Substance abuse is maladaptive use with adverse consequences including failure to fulfill major role obligations — which is physically hazardous and causes legal and social problems. Impairment, however, is less severe.

Abuse and dependence often involves several substances. Individuals who abuse cocaine often begin with drinking. Impulse control reduction results in cocaine use. Alcohol and other drugs are also often used in an attempt to counteract the anxiety related to cocaine withdrawal. Alcohol and cannabis are often used together. Associated features of drug abuse and dependence often include personality and mood disturbance. Antisocial behaviors can develop. Individuals who abuse drugs often display radical mood changes. During use and withdrawal, irritability, anger and anxiety are common. (Of course, this varies with individuals, the substance ingested and the pattern of use.) Alcohol abuse and dependence usually begin in the 20's and 30's. Women tend to develop dependence at a later age than men. Women also tend to drink alone and hide dependence as well as resist treatment. One of the real gains in treating chemical dependence among women is to recognize different needs in treatment and the development of programs taking cognizance of the different patterns of use and abuse as well as emotional and need differences.

Physical problems connected with prolonged alcohol abuse and dependence include hepatitis, cirrhosis, peripheral neuropathy, and gastritis as well as increased risk of heart disease, pneumonia, tuberculosis and neurological disorders.

Research suggests that children of those with psychoactive substance use disorders are predisposed for development themselves although debate as to genetic vs environmental causal factors continues. About 35 percent of the U.S. adult population abstains from alcohol; 55 percent drink fewer than 3 drinks a week; 11 percent consume an average of one ounce or more of alcohol a day. The prevalence of drinking for both males and females is highest in the 21–34 age group. Ten percent of those who drink consume 50 percent of the total alcohol produced.

There are three patterns of chronic abuse and dependence. One consists of daily intake of large amounts; a second of heavy drinking primarily on weekends; and the last, long periods of abstinence followed by binge drinking. One of the denials often used by those who are chemically dependent is that they "only drink on weekends" or can stop drinking for long periods of times. Others include the pronouncement that they "never miss work" or "drink only beer." Many people who have serious alcohol related problems do not miss work. Of course, performance is usually severely impaired. Society loses hundreds of millions of dollars of produced goods and services due to drug use, abuse and dependence, not to mention the cost of treating related physical and medical problems and the emotional trauma caused within the family by alcoholism.

While alcoholism is often associated with depression where individuals claim they drink to self-medicate and "feel better," recent research suggests that depression usually is secondary or a consequence rather than a cause of drinking. Research has not, however, proved either hypothesis and it is probable that both conditions exist. Many treatment programs are now addressing problems other than dependence per se, such as personality disorder traits and mood disorder which may be coexisting conditions.

The course of development with males and females appears to differ. Males commonly begin abuse earlier (late teens and early 20's) with dependence developing in the 30's. With females onset is usually later, with spontaneous remission less frequent. Tolerance appears to differ between individuals as well as races. A recent study reports that approximately 13 percent of the adult U.S. population has experienced alcohol abuse or dependence at some time in their lives.

Chapter VIII

ALCOHOL ABUSE AND DEPENDENCE— THE IMPACT ON THE FAMILY AND COPING TECHNIQUES

Adult Children of Alcoholics, Codependency and Enablement

Recently a great deal has been written about the impact on individuals who have grown up in homes where one or more of the parents is chemically dependent. Research has focused primarily on alcohol families. Adults who grew up in such an environment are labelled Adult Children of Alcoholics (ACOA). Support groups to deal with common problems and counseling models have been developed to treat symptoms, behaviors and attitudes claimed to have developed as the result of growing up in a dysfunctional family.

According to recent literature, ACOA attitudes and behaviors are related to the unstable, unpredictable and often chaotic nature of the environment in an alcoholic home. It is certainly true that in most cases there is a lack of adequate and accurate reality testing in such homes and families. Denial is one of the most common ways of attempting to deal with alcoholism. The chemically dependent individual usually denies dependence. Other family members also tend to deny the existence of problems. Thus, individuals from an alcoholic home tend to minimize problems, rationalize and deny in their own lives.

Individuals from alcoholic families also have been taught not to "cause problems" and express their true feelings. The enabler attempts to keep a calm and serene atmosphere in order to limit or eliminate stress in the home. "Stress" is "blamed" for the alcoholic's abuse or binges. Of course, this is only part of the story. Chemically dependent persons drink because they are chemically dependent not because of stress per se. In fact, recent studies suggest that the person who is chemically dependent often creates crisis to defocus from abuse or dependence. Nevertheless,

41

children in a dysfunctional home tend to keep their problems to themselves. They often are not aware of their emotions because they have been required to repress them. They also have problems disclosing their emotions.

Lack of trust in others is a problem with Adult Children of Alcoholics because of the lack of consistency during their early development years. Often the alcoholic parent is abusive at one time and overly loving another. Promises are often broken to the children. No wonder trust and intimacy are difficult with ACOA people.

ACOA literature identifies difficulty in following through on projects and tasks as another trait. This is probably due to distractions from task completion and often chaos in the home environment where plans were often changed or structure lacking. Some research indicates that Adult Children of Alcoholics have problems with careers because of a lack of consistency in effort.

Adult children tend to be very serious, have problems having fun and like to be in control. Approaches to life tend to be rigid with limited flexibility. These traits, again appear to be related to early childhood experiences including disappointments at the last moment, broken promises, and a parent or parents who appeared to be out of control. As was discussed, often one of the children become the "responsible parent." This individual (usually the oldest child or the oldest girl) tend to have real problems with joy, having fun and letting others share in decisions.

Adult children of alcoholics reportedly tend to overreact in situations where they have no control. Again, this is related to lack of trust that dependency and security needs will be met and the need to "fend for themselves." Adult children are often overly responsible, however there is evidence that some individuals have developed a coping mechanism of rebellion and irresponsibility. Often these are the younger children or the youngest child. Adult children appear to have problems with self-esteem. Often they have been abused (verbally as well as physically) and have a poor sense of self-worth. They have internalized criticism and negative messages about themselves. Depression is common. Abuse of alcohol and other mood altering drugs is common also (possibly because of genetic factors and possibly because of environmental causes). Self-abuse and participation in dangerous and self-defeating relationships and situations is not uncommon. These behaviors appear to be related to a poorly developed sense of self and low self-esteem.

Because love, attention and reinforcement were either missing or inconsistent in alcoholic families, many members develop an oversensitivity to the opinion of others and the need for acceptance and recognition. Alcoholic families tend to produce at least one workaholic or over achiever as well as individuals who are insecure and in need of inordinate attention or affection.

Adult children of alcoholics tend to focus on immediate satisfaction rather than postponement. They tend to overspend and make inadequate plans for the future. This, of course, reflects the fact that as children they often could not count on consistency. This focus on material needs suggests a basic insecurity and anxiety.

Twelve step programs can offer direction and help individuals make positive and significant changes in their behaviors and attitudes. Many adult children of alcoholics have become involved in an ACOA program. If you recognize some of the symptoms mentioned above, in yourself, you might consider participation in an ACOA group. These groups are confidential and participation is open-ended. On the other hand, groups are not a panacea. Many people seek professional therapy to deal with counterproductive and pathological attitudes and behaviors. On occasion, individuals become "addicted" to 12 step programs. These programs, just like therapy, should be used for personal growth and improvement, not as a substitute for "a real life." Also, there are many causes of mental and emotional problems. Individuals should be cautioned against "blaming" their childhood for their current life problems and situations.

We have discussed many of the adult symptoms related to growing up in an alcoholic family. At this time it seems appropriate to identify some behaviors which children currently in an alcoholic family display. Children in alcoholic homes are often tardy in school, especially on Monday mornings. They also commonly express concern about getting home immediately following school. Often they display signs of regression such as enuresis, thumb sucking, and immature social behavior. They tend to avoid arguments and conflict and are frequently ill. Frequent visits to the school nurse with vague somatic complaints or stomachaches are common. Children living in an alcoholic home tend to be isolative and usually resist having playmates come home with them. Fatigue, listlessness and poor school attendance are also common.

Living in an alcoholic family is difficult. Codependence and enabling behaviors are common among family members. Codependency is a continuing pattern of overdependence on the person who is chemically dependent. (In this discussion we will focus on chemical dependency —

codependency, although other forms of codependence exist such as in a love relationship, or with a sick or disabled individual. Parent/child codependency with problems in separation and emancipation also exists.) Codependence is characterized by preoccupation with and extreme dependence on the other person for one's happiness. Individuals who are codependent require approval and acceptance by the other person. They attempt to provide for the other person by solving their problems or relieving their pain. Their focus is on pleasing and protecting the other person. They lack self-esteem and "feel good" about themselves only when the other person reinforces them. Their happiness depends on the other person. They lack internal resources to make themselves happy. The desires of the other person dictate their attitudes and behaviors. Their dreams for the future are linked to another. They allow themselves to be manipulated because of fear of rejection. Their social activities and the quality of their life is dependent on the other person.

Of course, these attitudes and behaviors are self-defeating and counter-productive. Individual needs are never met because the focus is on the other person. In an alcoholic relationship, codependency is especially damaging. Often the alcoholic resents the relationship and becomes abusive. Denial is reinforced because the codependent will not confront the alcoholic or identify problems. Codependence tends to have a negative impact on other members of the family because relationships are not developed and needs met. Resentments, conflicts and jealousy are common. Codependency treatment programs have been developed and might be considered if you or one of your family members suffers from the related problems. These programs often include education and lectures on codependency, group therapy, individual and family therapy, psychological testing, a medical evaluation, involvement in a twelve step program, stress control and management, education, and assertiveness training.

Enabling behaviors are defined as behaviors which allow the alcoholic to continue use and abuse. These behaviors tend to relieve the chemically dependent individual of responsibility. It is common for a codependent or other family member to become an enabler. Just as in codependency, these behaviors and responses tend to perpetuate the problem. Specific examples of enabling include calling school or work for the individual because they are intoxicated or experiencing withdrawal; "covering up" in social situations or making excuses to relatives and neighbors for missed obligations; minimizing ("He or she is under a lot of stress" or

"There are others who drink a lot more"); taking over responsibilities; rescuing ("I couldn't let him sit in jail"); enduring ("Maybe he'll get better when he gets employment or changes his job") and failing to take positive actions to satisfy one's own needs or change the situation.

Involvement in a twelve step program such as Alanon or Family Anonymous (FA) might be considered. These groups are for family members and help develop healthy coping mechanisms. It allows participants to focus on themselves and their own needs as well as to realize that they did not cause the alcoholism. They cannot control it and they cannot cure it. Detachment with love is suggested. Individuals are encouraged to identify their own feelings and express them. Support from others is provided. Many of these issues and "steps" can also be explored in individual and family therapy.

Treatment for alcoholism and other forms of chemical dependence has improved greatly in recent years. Intensive outpatient care where the individual lives at home and continues work is a current and very effective trend in treating chemical dependence. Insurance coverage is often available. Family participation in treatment allows for members to resolve personal issues related to their own problems, feelings and emotions. Participation in Alcoholics Anonymous is also often recommended for the individual who is chemically dependent.

Many of the techniques mentioned in the first section of this book are applicable for use by family members who are impacted by alcoholism in the family. Others have been mentioned in this chapter such as involvement in a support group, and individual and family therapy. Intervention is also often suggested to overcome denial and help the alcoholic realize the need for treatment.

This final section contains very practical and specific ways to deal with alcoholism. First, responses that will *not* work include:

1) Denial.
2) Home treatment remedies, which are attempts to "remove" the problems personally. These "remedies" include statements such as "If you loved me you would quit" and "Why don't you use your will power." Other remedies include threatening without action, coaxing, pleading, and hiding or destroying alcohol.
3) A martyred attitude.
4) Accepting lies.
5) Lecturing and scolding.

6) Arguing.
7) Accepting promises in order to postpone pain.
8) Enabling and allowing one's self to be exploited.

Responses that *do* work include:

1) Learning all the facts about alcoholism and researching treatment programs.
2) Taking care of self. Attending support groups and considering individual therapy.
3) Keep emotionally detached. This is difficult but vital.
4) Confront the alcoholic in a nonemotional, nonjudgemental way.
5) Become involved in your own interests and build new relationships.
6) Identify your own needs and plan for the future.
7) Do not enable.
8) Refuse to tolerate abuse.
9) Take responsibility for yourself but not for the alcoholic.
10) If you make any threats be prepared to carry through on them.

Chapter IX

ADOLESCENT DRUG ABUSE AND DEPENDENCY

This chapter on adolescents and drug use, abuse and dependence has been included for two reasons. First, because of the prevalence of drug use and abuse among adolescents and secondly because of the serious negative impact on family as well as the adolescent.

Contrary to recent hopeful reports by some sectors, including agencies charged with fighting the war on drugs, adolescent use of drugs has not been significantly reduced. There have been some changes in use; however abuse is still a major and very serious problem. A recent study of teenage use has revealed that adolescents continue to use and abuse alcohol at an early age. Use of cocaine as an inhalant has decreased; however a more powerful and addictive form of cocaine (crack) is becoming available. Use of cannabis continues to be a major problem. Adolescents are also beginning to use inhalants such as glue, gasoline and cleaning fluid and hallucinogens such as phencyclidine (PCP) more frequently. Alcohol use and abuse continues. Education as to dangers of drug use and abuse have not solved the problem. Attempts to limit supplies of drugs have been ineffective. Drugs are available in schools, at work and in play areas.

A 1990 study concluded that almost 20 percent of all teenagers have had 5 or more drinks of alcohol on at least one occasion within the last two weeks. Ten percent of children 9 to 12 stated that cocaine or crack were "easy to get" in their area. Fifteen percent stated that they have been approached to buy drugs. Twenty percent of children ages 9 to 12 use alcohol or cigarettes. Forty-one percent of the high school seniors surveyed have, on one or more occasions, smoked cannabis. Nine percent admitted to cocaine use. These figures are shocking not only because of the frequency of use but also because of the availability of drugs.

While there are groups that stress abstinence and programs such as Operation Snowball that educate, there appears to be a great deal of peer pressure to use drugs. Parties and social events often include use of alcohol with other drugs available. Adolescence is a time when individuals seek peer approval. Refusal to experiment with drugs or "join in" sometimes results in fears of rejection. Parental prohibition is often tempered with fears that the adolescent will not be accepted and will be excluded from social events.

Adolescence is a difficult time developmentally. The individual is dealing with issues of identity and value formation. A sense of self has not been fully developed. Identity and self-esteem are often related to external factors such as peer acceptance, being "cool" and being a part of the "in group." Adolescence is also a time of separation and individuation. Adolescents must prepare themselves for emancipation. Development of career skills as well as social abilities is a major task. This is a time when relationships with the opposite sex become significant. There are a number of decisions and choices to be made which will affect one's life for a significant period of time. Abuse of drugs interferes not only with daily functioning but also with the development of emotional maturity. Individuals versed in treating adolescent drug abuse and dependence claim that social as well as emotional development is fixated or arrested at the age stage when the individual begins to abuse drugs. There appears to be some evidence to support this. Certainly social skills, the ability to deal with stress, motivation, impulse control and self-responsibility are not adequately developed.

Adolescents who abuse drugs usually have academic problems. Failure and dropping out of school is common. There is also evidence that drug use increases the risk for gang membership, involvement in illegal activities, and teenage pregnancy. Teenage intoxication and traffic deaths are commonly related. Every high school in every town has experienced one or more tragic events having to do with teenage drug abuse. Studies indicate that a significant number of teenage suicides involve the use of drugs. Drugs tend to impair judgement, reasoning and reality testing. Risk taking becomes more prevalent. Sexual promiscuity and antisocial behaviors are more common when under the influence of drugs.

Common symptoms or behaviors associated with adolescent drug use and abuse include:

1) Withdrawal, secretiveness and isolation.
2) A change in peer group.
3) A low tolerance for frustration, irritability and radical mood swings.
4) Problems with concentration.
5) Academic problems. Withdrawal from school activities.

6) Lethargy and lack of interest in activities which previously provided enjoyment.
7) Rebellion and resentment of authority.
8) Sudden disappearance of money or valuables from home.
9) Involvement in risk type activities.
10) Legal problems.
11) Use of drug terminology and possession of drug paraphenalia.
12) Chronic dry, irritating cough, or sore throat.

Certainly some of these symptoms can be related to causes other than drug use. Anxiety and depression can cause many of the symptoms mentioned above; however the presence of a significant number of the symptoms should be cause for concern. An evaluation should be considered. Urine and blood tests are of some value; however a drug use assessment by a certified addiction counselor or therapist trained in chemical dependency is usually the first step. Many treatment centers offer free evaluations as do a number of community service agencies. The schools are becoming more aware of adolescent drug use related problems and often can be of assistance in directing the family to qualified and capable professionals.

Chemical dependency among adolescents tends to be more debilitating than with the adult population. Adolescents often have not developed a sense of identity and adequate impulse and emotional controls. Judgement is often inadequate because of lack of experience. Many teenagers use drugs indiscriminately with the intention of becoming intoxicated or "high." Adolescents who are emotionally vulnerable tend to use drugs "to feel better" or self-medicate. Drugs are often used as an escape. Adolescents who sell drugs report a sense of power and feeling of importance. Often parents and counselors "accept" drug use, rationalizing that this is a part of "growing up." However, drugs are more available and more powerful than in the 1960's and the impact more severe.

There are four stages of adolescent abuse. Recognition of these stages is important in order to develop a treatment plan and assess the level of severity. The first stage is recreational use. This stage often begins in junior high school, and involves drinking beer, experimenting with cannabis and possibly using inhalants. Individuals report a sense of excitement. The need to be accepted and not labelled in a negative way is a primary factor in experimentation.

Social and recreational use is the second stage. Use is more regular.

Liquor is often used. Tolerance begins to develop as well as symptoms such as truancy, hangovers and irresponsibility. Experimentation with hallucinogens is common at this stage. Parents often notice a change in friendships, secretiveness and the need for money. There are attempts to hide the effects of drugs and a tendency to become irritable and moody.

The third stage is one of increased preoccupation with drugs and use. Antisocial traits, attitudes and behaviors become more evident. Hygiene and personal care tend to deteriorate. Rebellion increases with running away common. Often the adolescent becomes involved with the law. Symptoms of depression tend to develop. Suicidal ideations are often expressed.

The fourth stage is dependence with more severe impairment in functional abilities, risk of irreversible brain damage and severe physical and emotional problems. Drugs have robbed many adolescents of opportunities to develop socially and emotionally and enter adulthood with hope and feelings of well being and security.

It is beyond the scope of this book to provide an indepth discussion of the various mood altering drugs however alcohol, cannabis, inhalants, PCP, "crack" and "designer drugs" will be discussed briefly. Alcohol and cannabis are the most widely used drugs among teenagers. Inhalants and "designer drugs" as well as crack cocaine are considered to be the most potent and dangerous drugs. These three drugs as well as PCP are beginning to enter the adolescent drug culture. The possibility for neurological and physiological injury and damage, the availability and the potency of these drugs are cause for serious consideration and concern.

Alcohol is a central nervous system depressant. It can be psychologically and physically addicting. The cost to society, both financially and emotionally, is enormous. Teenage drinking is of concern not only because of the addictive possibilities but the developmental/social/family problems related to abuse. Use of alcohol often leads to use of other drugs. Teenage suicide and death is also related to alcohol abuse. Mortality rates have decreased among all age groups except for 15–24 year olds. The leading cause of death in this age group is drunk and drugged driving. Traffic accidents are the leading cause of violent deaths with 50 percent of these accident involving use of alcohol.

Marijuana is a derivative of the cannabis plant. There are more than 400 known chemical parts to the plant, however one of these (delta-9-tetrahydrocannabinol also referred to as THC) is the primary mood altering ingredient. Initially marijuana was considered a harmless recreational drug providing a sense of well being or euphoria. However, recent research implies that use can produce adverse effects on health. It is now recognized that even low doses of marijuana can adversely affect driving performance, judgement and perceptive ability. In some users a single dose can produce adversive reactions from anxiety to paranoia and panic. Heavy use tends to impair the ability to concentrate as well as memory and learning. Amotivational syndrome has been identified in adolescents with a tendency to be poorly motivated. Anhedonia is also common.

Cannabis is usually smoked. Cannabis produces 50 percent more tar than the same quantity of tobacco. The concentration of carcinogens (cancer producing agents) is 70 percent higher in marijuana than in a cigarette. Since smoke from a "joint" is inhaled more deeply and retained in the lungs for a longer period of time, 2 or 3 cannabis cigarettes a day carry the same risk of lung damage as a pack of cigarettes. (More disturbing is that the marijuana available today as compared to 10 years ago is 25 times more potent. There is also a greater prevalence of other agents such as PCP in the drug.) Cardiovascular problems with increased heart rate have been reported as well as problems in fertility and sexual potency. Another major concern is damage to the offspring of cannabis users due to the toxic effect of the drug during pregnancy. High doses of THC also tend to reduce the efficiency of the immune system.

PCP is a hallucinogenic drug. It is often referred to as "angel dust," "TIC" or "TAC." It results in increased blood pressure, lack of coordination, loss of sensitivity to pain, and imprecise eye movements. Behavioral signs of use include withdrawal, confusion, disorientation, bizarre behavior, aggressiveness and hyperactivity alternating with stupor. Rage episodes and complete loss of emotional control with a tendency for violence and self destruction are not uncommon. Recent studies report an increase among adolescents of PCP, especially in conjunction with other drugs.

Inhalants have also increased in adolescent use. Substances include glue, gasoline, deodorants and other aerosols, and typewriter correction fluid. The use of inhalants is not restricted in the controlled substance act of 1970 so there are no federal penalties for possession or sale of these substances. A number of states have passed laws to prohibit sale to adolescents; however, the variety of substances and availability is so intensive that legal prohibition cannot restrict use. The primary route of administration is inhalation. Liquids are often soaked into a cloth and inhaled. Aerosols are commonly sprayed into a paper bag for inhalation. While the effect varies from agent to agent, most inhalants produce central nervous system depression. The primary risks are death, organic brain damage, kidney damage, liver damage, leukemia and paralysis.

"Designer drugs" are substances created scientifically to mimic the effect of controlled substances and sold on the illicit market. A brief discussion of this class of drugs is included because of the potency of the drugs and the tendency for adolescents who abuse drugs and are "part of the drug culture" for indiscriminate use in order to experience new and more extensive states of euphoria. Because of potency, synergesic reactions with other drugs and contaminants overdosing is common.

"Crack" while not a designer drug is an example of increased potency of a substance. Cocaine is normally inhaled as a powder, smoked or administered intravenously. The last two forms of ingestion are most effective as far as impact and speed of reaction. "Freebasing" is the process of removing the carrier or dilutant from cocaine in order to obtain a more powerful substance and be able to smoke the drug. This requires preparation and special paraphernalia. Crack is cocaine in rock form rather than powder form and can be smoked without preparation. Crack is extremely addictive. New data indicates that an adolescent can become addicted within a few weeks or months of initial use. Symptoms of cocaine use include nasal irritation, dilated pupils, rapid respiration, and hyperactivity. Behavioral signs are rapid mood swings, lack of money due to the cost of the drug, problems with concentration and functional disability.

Adolescent drug abuse tends to have a severe impact on the family. Often the parents are shocked, angry and confused. Self-blame is common. Other family members are also impacted by the disorder. Siblings are often confused and angry. In many cases the adolescent's attitude and behavior have caused family conflict and disunity. Financial and legal problems which cause family stress may have developed. In any case, adolescent drug abuse and dependence creates crisis and trauma in the family system. This must be considered and appreciated when taking action. Three principles are important.

1) Seek expert advise. Many agencies and treatment facilities will provide a free evaluation and help the family develop a logical and effective treatment program.
2) Involve the family. Take care of your own needs, as well as the

needs of family members. Often the "patient" becomes the focus with other family members suffering.

3) Act decisively. Early intervention is important. Denial, enabling behavior and postponement of confrontation only delay treatment and recovery.

Chapter X

ALZHEIMER'S

Dementia of the Alzheimer's Type

There are two types of Alzheimer's disease according to *DSM IV*. One type occurs after age 65 and is referred to as late onset of the Alzheimer. The other occurs prior to age 65 and is referred to as early onset. Both types can be debilitating and severely impair functional ability.

In this chapter we will focus on the symptoms, diagnosis and coping/treatment issues rather than the age of onset although late onset is more common than early onset. With the graying of America and increased life spans we in the mental health field are seeing an increase in Alzheimer's disease. Dementia is present in up to 9 percent of people over 65 and is becoming a major health issue as the percentage of individuals over 65 is reaching 12 percent of the population. Alzheimer's disease itself is a physical disorder. In our discussion we will focus primarily on dementia in terms of intellectual abilities, behaviors and emotions.

The essential feature of dementia of the Alzheimer type is of multiple cognitive deficits. The onset is insidious and the course progressive with increased impairment and disability. The symptoms can include impairment in memory and inability to learn new information and one or more of the following: language disturbance, inability to perform motor tasks, inability to identify objects, and poor planning, abstract thinking and disorganization. Dementia can be mild where work and social activities are impaired but the family member can live independently with adequate hygiene and relatively intact judgement. Or impairment may be more severe where independent living is hazardous or so impaired that continual supervision is required. In late stage Alzheimer's, the person is unable to maintain minimal hygiene and is incoherent or mute.

The diagnosis of dementia is primary. This is because up to 34 percent of the cases diagnosed are treatable and indeed not organic in nature. (Recent studies have suggested that 11 percent of all cases diagnosed are not cases of dementia.) A neuropsychological assessment is strongly recommended. Casual factors which can be treated include emotional problems (especially depression), nutrition, drug toxicity (including toxicity related to overmedication on prescription medication), and hydroencephalitis. Nontreatable dementias include those which are organic such as vascular dementia, brain trauma, and specific diseases such as Huntington's chorea and Korsakoff's syndrome. Often history, physical examination or laboratory tests for a specific organic factor are not conclusive. This is one reason that an intellectual and behavioral assessment is recommended, i.e., to evaluate the possibility that the dementia is treatable. Organic causes are probable when there is a loss of a specific mental ability, there are consistent behavioral deficits (such as inability to remember any childhood events or learn new information), inappropriate affect, lack of awareness of problems or focus on trivial matters. Diffuse problems, motivational problems, symptoms of anxiety and/or depression, extreme mood swings, and awareness of deficits can be signs of pseudodementia or dementia which is not related to organic causes.

Individuals who are suffering from dementia of the Alzheimer type can also have delusions, be depressed, and suffer from delirium. Depressive factors and delusions complicate diagnosis and treatment.

Late onset dementia (after age 65) is more common than early onset. Age of onset is seldom prior to age 50. The first stages of dementia are usually memory loss with such personality changes as apathy, lack of enthusiasm and withdrawal following. Often there is anger and irritation. As the disease progresses, functional abilities deteriorate. The average duration of the disorder from onset to death is about five years.

Brain atrophy is considered a primary causal factor in Alzheimer's disease. Computer assisted tomography or pneumdencephalography may be used in diagnosis. Senile plaques, neurofibrillary tangles and neuron degeneration are commonly discovered. However, there are many neurological and organic similarities in the normal aging brain compared to the brain of an individual with Alzheimer's disorder. The advantage of a neuropsychological evaluation is that areas of impairment (intellectual, emotional and functional) can be assessed and treatment and management decisions made.

Down's syndrome is a predisposing factor in Alzheimer's disease. Between 2 percent to 4 percent of the population will probably develop Alzheimer's with the incidence increasing after age 75. The disorder is more common in females and there appears to be a genetic factor in the disorder. Many elderly individuals present with symptoms of dementia. Often these individuals are suffering from situational and/or life stage factors and indeed are not demented. Again this is why an accurate assessment is important. The diagnosis of Alzheimer's must be limited to situations where there is evidence of dementia with a progressive deteriorating course and the exclusion of all other specific causes of dementia.

At this time, no effective treatment has been discovered or developed to reverse cognitive impairments such as memory loss or the inability to learn new information, tasks and functions. However, research has improved management techniques and developed medication approaches to overcome some of the behavioral problems and symptoms so that the patient can feel calmer and more in control. Antipsychotic drugs are often prescribed to control delusions, paranoia, agitation, violence and verbal outbursts. Use of such medication can delay an individual's entry into a nursing home or institution.

While there appear to be benefits in using medication to improve behavior and secondary symptoms of Alzheimer's, these techniques are often not utilized. Recent studies showed that among patients on antipsychotic medication, the drugs completely controlled behavioral symptoms in one-third of the population, produced moderate improvement in one-third and had no significant impact on the remaining third.

Of course, medication must be prescribed and monitored by a physician. A number of considerations must be taken into account in treating an elderly patient with Alzheimer's. Often the elderly are overmedicated. Synergetic impact from a variety of medications can create serious problems. There is also the issue of medical compliance. Medication must be supervised in the case of an individual with memory problems. The elderly also tend to have a lower metabolism and dosages must be adjusted. Family members should be very particular in choosing a physician when considering medical interventions. Experience in treating geriatric patients as well as mental disorders is advised. Response to medication must be monitored.

Antipsychotic drugs will not reverse the progressive deterioration of the brain. Consequently the family is advised to consider ways of dealing with the patient that will be beneficial for the family as well as the individual with Alzheimer's. Understanding the nature of the disorder and the emotional impact on the individual who is suffering from Alzheimer's is a first step in providing for the individual's needs in a loving and caring way. Family members must realize that in the early stages of Alzheimer's the patient is usually aware of changes in abilities including memory, learning and functioning. The changes are more than "a slow down" in ability or lack of physical strength. The changes include confusion and impaired reasoning and problem solving ability. Simple tasks such as paying bills, shopping, food preparation and personal hygiene become difficult because of deteriorating mental ability.

Often the individual in the early stages of Alzheimer's attempts to hide problems. They may confabulate or withdraw from family. Usually, during the early stages of Alzheimer's there develops a irritability. This is based primarily on frustration and feelings of inadequacy, impotence and fear. The fear is related to not understanding what is going on and the impairment in abilities that once were intact. Often there is a level of anxiety. Depression is common. These emotional responses of course tend to exacerbate problems.

Family members and caretakers must be aware of these emotions. Often the behavior of someone with Alzheimer's is abusive and seemingly irrational, however the behavior is, at least during early stages of Alzheimer's, based on anxiety, fear, depression and confusion. Providing a sense of security; performing tasks for the impaired family member without insulting the individual's integrity and sense of independence; being patient, loving and non-confrontive; and planning for future needs are all ways of helping the individual cope with Alzheimer's. Limited stimulation has also been suggested. Large family parties or gatherings, unplanned visits and changes in living arrangements tend to increase anxiety with possible decompensation and regression. Repetition will be necessary in giving instructions and in performing tasks in that memory deficits impede new learning and task performance. Often individuals with Alzheimer's retain some ability to read although comprehension is limited. Writing the day of the week and the month, as well as simple instructions can provide a sense of orientation.

Discussions of plans for future care can create anxiety, often more for the caretaker than the individual with Alzheimer's. Assurance that the individual's independence and well being will be respected and that the least restrictive form of care provided will lessen the anxiety. However, it is important that the family as well as the individual with Alzheimer's be realistic about the eventual need for intensive care.

The above mentioned intervention and management techniques and strategies can help in dealing with a family member with Alzheimer's. The focus of the discussion so far has been on the "patient." Now we shall discuss in more detail the impact on the family and ways to cope. Alzheimer's disease can have a devastating effect on the family both financially and emotionally.

Family conflict can develop when one of the adult children is required to assume a major share of the responsibility in the care of an elderly parent with Alzheimer's. Often one person (sometimes because of logistics—sometimes not) is placed in a position where he or she must devote a major portion of time to the care of a parent. In our society, with an aging population, middle age individuals often have burdens and responsibilities related to caring for their own children as well as their parents. This often creates tension and resentment.

In other cases, the spouse is expected or attempts to care for a partner with Alzheimer's. This can create physical problems in situations where the elderly spouse is limited in providing care as well as emotional problems.

The progressive and degenerative element of Alzheimer's compounds emotional problems. Often family members experience feelings of guilt as well as resentment, anger and sadness. It is not unusual to become exasperated, physically drained and emotionally overwhelmed, especially when there are unresolved issues from the past. Role reversals with the child becoming the parent can be a stressful situation. Often the family member goes through a time of reviewing past experiences. If there has not been resolution of painful situations and events there is a tendency for past resentments to grow and cause feelings of dysphoria. This, of course, complicates the situation in the present time.

Personality changes associated with Alzheimer's can also create stress and emotional problems. At a time, for example, when an adult child may wish to resolve issues and relate to a parent with Alzheimer's the patient may be unable to understand or respond in an appropriate way. The spouse of an individual with Alzheimer's is dealing with additional issues including their own aging and future.

Each family will experience different dynamics when a member develops Alzheimer's, just as the impact of the disorder will be different, depending on the relationship, roles and rules within the family system. Many of the techniques in coping with mental illness, in the previous chapters, apply, however other more specific suggestions include:

1) A neuropsychological assessment in order to determine the nature of the disorder and possible interventions. Cognitive, behavioral and functional abilities should be evaluated and plans for the future made.

As was discussed, many forms of dementia are treatable. Others are manageable.

2) Involve family members. Discuss expectations, obligations and practical matters related to finances, time, and energy each family or family member is willing to be responsible for in the caretaking process.

3) Consider the emotional impact on one's self and other family members. This might be an appropriate time for family members to come together and share memories and past experiences. Research suggests that "life reviews" and sharing feelings and emotions often helps in resolving loss and dealing with grief. Certainly the loss of mental abilities, personality changes and functional disability of a loved family member creates emotional dysphoria and must be addressed. Professional help might be helpful.

4) Take advantage of community services. Often there are agencies and groups that will help relieve the pain and strain of dealing with a family member with Alzheimer's. Primary caretakers, in particular, must realize that they too need relief and time away to care for their own needs and physical and mental health. In late stage Alzheimer's, institutional care is often required. Making this decision is often difficult. Realizing that the individual in the late stages of Alzheimer's does not have the intellectual ability or the emotional capacity to feel and comprehend may ease your pain and allow for you, as a family member, to realize that such a decision is necessary.

Chapter XI

ATTENTION DEFICIT
HYPERACTIVITY DISORDER

It is estimated that 2.5 million children in the United States have Attention deficit hyperactivity disorder (ADHD). Five percent of school age children suffer from ADHD, 90 percent of ADHD children are underachievers in school. Boys out number girls 5 to 1. ADHD is not the result of "bad parenting"; however recent research has suggested that there is a family genetic predisposition for ADHD. (According to the National Institute of Health at least some of the cases are triggered by a heredity error that causes an uncommon endocrine disorder called generalized resistance to thyroid hormone.)

Individuals with ADHD often develop academic and behavioral problems. Thirty percent of the children with ADHD have failed at least one year of high school. Thirty-five percent of the adolescents with ADHD never complete high school. Thirty percent of the ADHD children have speech, learning or language problems. The U.S. Department of Education has recognized ADHD as a disability and requires schools to provide appropriate services. And ADHD is treatable.

ADHD is a developmental disorder. There are three types: A combined type which includes symptoms of inattention and hyperactivity; a type which is predominately inattentive; and a third type where the individual is predominately hyperactive and impulsive. The combined type is the most common type. Often, individuals who are inattentive and not hyperactive, unfortunately are not diagnosed. Some researchers, including this author, are of the opinion that many children and adolescents who are having academic and behavioral problems, are suffering from ADD rather than specific speech, language and learning problems. Remediation has not been provided because they are not as obvious as the child who is hyperactive.

Children with ADHD often develop behavioral problems. ADHD children are difficult to raise as well as teach. Their lack of attention and impulsiveness is usually considered volitional. Often inability to attend and control impulses is disruptive in class as well as home. Relationships with peers and siblings are often poor because ADHD children tend to act without emotional control. They tend to be noisy and impetuous. These children are often labelled early in life as "the class clown" or as "the class trouble maker." This can turn into a self-fulfilling prophecy. Soon the individual is disciplined rather than helped. It is not uncommon for the child to be rejected by peers and develop feelings of inadequacy and low self-esteem. Problems with academics (usually not because of impaired intelligence but because of the lack of the ability to attend and control their impulses) often results in discipline, ridicule and a sense of failure. Family conflict develops because of school problems and inability to "behave" at home. Severe depression is not uncommon. As the individual becomes older, antisocial acting out is common with the risk of school dropout, sexual promiscuity, gang membership, association with negative peers, drug abuse and legal problems. Unfortunately individuals usually do not "outgrow" ADHD. Adults with ADHD commonly have problems learning, problems career-wise and relationship problems. However, there is hope. As was stated, there is effective treatment for ADHD. However, an accurate diagnosis and intervention is primary.

Symptoms of ADHD include:

Short attention span	Restlessness
Academic problems	Acts before thinking
Impulsivity	Difficulty staying seated
Excessive physical movement	Talking out of turn
Daydreaming	Fidgeting
Problems with task completion	Problems following rules
Discipline problems	Difficulty with peers and siblings
Poorly organized work	Problems with sustained effort
Ease of distraction	Interrupting
Sloppy, incomplete work	Does not seem to listen

ADHD can be mild (with few of the symptoms), moderate with impairment in functional ability and severe with significant impaired functioning at home, in school and with peers.

The symptoms tend to be present in most situations; however they are more severe at times of stress and when sustained attention is required, such as in test situations. (This is one reason why individuals with

ADHD do so poorly on tests.) In one to one settings, when provided with reinforcement and when structure, direction and control are provided performance tends to improve. Problems with peers often develop at an early age because of impulsivity. Children with ADHD tend to have problems waiting for their turn. They often do not follow rules and tend to grab objects and toys from others. Engaging in potentially dangerous activities such as skateboard riding in traffic or rough terrain is also common.

In preschool children, hypermotor activity is an early symptom, such as excessive running and climbing. Older individuals tend to fidget and be restless. (As was discussed, children with predominately inattentive type do not display these signs of hyperactivity.) Associated features include low self-esteem, radical mood changes, a low tolerance for frustration and temper tantrums as well as academic underachievement.

Although research suggests that 50 percent of the cases of ADHD develop before age four, frequently the disorder is not recognized until the individual enters school. And, often, an accurate diagnosis is not made until much later, if ever. This is one of the primary problems. By the time ADHD is diagnosed behavioral, academic, family and emotional problems have usually developed.

In the majority of cases of ADHD the disorder continues through childhood. Often Oppositional Defiant and/or Conduct Disorder develops. Antisocial Personality Disorder in adulthood is common. Studies show that approximately one-third of the children with ADHD continue to have symptoms in adulthood.

A genetic factor has been identified; however research also suggests other predisposing factors such as central nervous system abnormalities, disorganized or chaotic environments, and/or child abuse and neglect. In making a diagnosis age appropriate overactivity must be ruled out. Some children are hyperactive but do not suffer from attention, memory and concentration problems. Some mood disorders also present as ADHD in that children who are depressed or anxious tend to have problems with concentration and memory.

ADHD has a tendency to disrupt a family. Behavioral problems, acting out and school failure are considered to be volitional. Punishment often does not help. The child tends to rebel and acting out increases. Feelings of depression, rejection and failure can result in withdrawal, isolation and in extreme cases suicidal ideations. The individual commonly has feelings of guilt and remorse over family conflict and academic failure, however tends to lack the ability to make adaptive changes.

Treatment includes education, medication and usually psychotherapy to address the behavioral, emotional and family problems. An accurate assessment is vital. This assessment should be made by a professional such as a child psychiatrist or psychologist who has experience with child development. A behavioral as well as intellectual and emotional evaluation is recommended. While many agencies provide parental and/or school "check lists" or inventories to screen for ADHD, a more complete and accurate assessment is needed. School or educational specialists should also provide a speech, language and learning evaluation so other developmental problems can be identified.

A number of medications have been developed to treat ADHD. These are primarily central nervous system stimulants. Side effects should be considered and of course the prescription and monitoring of the medication must be under the supervision of a physician.

The behavioral and emotional problems that are related to ADHD will possibly require professional help. These problems commonly include depression, drug abuse, antisocial personality tendencies, problems with social skills, lack of motivation and a failure identity.

Professional help can also provide parents with advice on how to help a child or adolescent with ADHD in the home environment. Individuals with ADHD respond best to structure, order, and positive reinforcement. Unity in parenting is vital. Other behavioral methods and techniques include writing down instructions, breaking tasks into smaller components, elimination of distractions (such as TV or music during study time), patience, taking time to listen, face-to-face communication (listening skills are often poor with individuals with ADHD) and keeping rules simple and specific.

Parents, teachers and counselors must coordinate efforts. Copies of the psychological, neuropsychological and speech, language and learning assessments should be utilized in developing a treatment as well as a academic remediation plan. If these recommendations are taken, the prognosis is good. Unfortunately, failure to recognize and treat ADHD often results in more severe emotional and behavioral problems. As was stated, most people do not "out grow" ADHD however with a combination of education, medication and psychotherapy treatment is effective.

Summary of specific recommendations for dealing with suspected ADHD:

1) An accurate evaluation. This includes a complete physical/medical examination to rule out such things as hyperthyroid disorder and hypoglycemia. A psychological and/or neuropsychological evaluation is also required. Contact a qualified professional who has experience in child development and in the assessment of behavior as well as emotional and intellectual factors. Finally, a speech, language and learning evaluation is recommended.

2) Once a diagnosis is made, develop a treatment plan with the assistance of an expert. There are many qualified sources for guidance. Community services may direct you to a qualified case manager. Hospitals and outpatient counseling services offer help. Individual counselors with a background in ADHD are also available. Often insurance will help cover the cost of an assessment as well as treatment, especially if the child or adolescent is also suffering from depression.

3) Coordinate efforts of family, school, and professional service providers. A physician will need to be involved to prescribe and monitor medication.

4) Realize that ADHD, while often impairing learning and resulting in acting out and inappropriate behavior, is not an indication of low mental abilities. In fact, many children with ADHD are extremely bright. With treatment these abilities can be developed and the child or adolescent with ADHD can live a rich, full, happy life. Behavior management techniques learned in counseling can and usually will result in parental unity and the development of a more supportive and functional family system for the benefit of all family members.

Chapter XII

EATING DISORDERS AND OBESITY

(Anorexia Nervosa and Bulimia)

D*SM IV* identifies a number of eating disorders, all of them characterized by disturbances in eating behavior. Two of these disorders,
pica and rumination disorder of infancy, are primarily disorders of
infancy and early childhood and will not be discussed. Anorexia nervosa
and bulimia are adolescent/adult disorders and will be focused on in this
chapter. Obesity is considered a physical disorder rather than a psychological or mental disorder although many theorists suggest that there is
an emotional causal factor in many cases of obesity. This chapter contains a brief discussion of obesity as well as anorexia and bulimia.

Anorexia nervosa is defined as the refusal to maintain body weight
over a minimal normal weight for age and height. The individual either
loses weight or, in the case of an adolescent, fails to gain weight. This
weight loss or failure to gain must be 15 percent below the normal age
height level.

The second criteria for anorexia is an intense fear of weight gain. A
third is a disturbance in body image. Individuals tend to consider
themselves overweight or to consider a certain part of the body "overweight." In women, three consecutive menstrual cycles must have been
missed.

There are two types of anorexia nervosa: the binge eating type and the
restricting type without binge/purge behavior.

Individuals suffering from anorexia initially tend to be preoccupied
with food as well as body weight. Loss of appetite is usually rare until late
in the illness. There is evidence that individuals who are anorexic are
constantly thinking about food. They often have a passion for collecting
recipes and a preoccupation with making and preparing food for others.
Most of their weight loss behaviors occur in secret. They tend to refuse to
eat with others at home and in public places. Weight loss is controlled by
a gross reduction in intake. Excessive exercise is also common. Frequently,

there is also self-induced vomiting and use of laxatives. Many individuals who are anorexic also suffer from bulimia nervosa.

Anorexia nervosa appears to be predominantly a female disorder although between 4 and 6 percent of the people who are anorexic are male. Age of onset is usually between thirteen and twenty although recent research suggests an increase in prepubertal adolescents as well as women over the age of thirty. About 8 million Americans are believed to have the disorder. Bulimia and anorexia kill about 6 percent of the people who have the disorder. The course of the disorder may be episodic; however more often it consists of a single episode. Hospitalization is frequently required to prevent death by starvation.

There appears to be a familial pattern to the disorder. Anorexia is more common among sisters and mothers of patients with the disorder than among the general population.

In some cases a particular psychosocial stressor such as a death in the family, or a divorce, precipitates or proceeds the episode. Individuals with the disorder have often been described as overly concerned with success and order, perfectionists, overly sensitive to the opinions of others and rigid in their approach to life. It is interesting that often obsessive compulsive behaviors develop after the onset of anorexia or that these behaviors are observed as concurrent and coexisting. Such activities as ritualistic exercising, running and cycling are common among anorectics.

Poor sexual adjustment is also frequently present. A marked disinterest in sex is common. There is also evidence of a significantly higher prevalence of suicide attempts, self-mutilation and substance abuse among those suffering from the disorder than in the general population. Many anorectics display symptoms of depression and indeed are depressed. These symptoms include sleep disturbance, crying spells, isolation and withdrawal from social contact and anhedonia. Physical problems related to vomiting and purging can include lower serum potassium levels leading to cardiac problems, erosion of the enamel of teeth and dental problems, and esophageal and gastric ruptures and damage. Amenorrhea is a major physical sign of anorexia and often appears before a noticeable weight loss.

There has been a great deal of speculation regarding the etiology of eating disorders and anorexia nervosa in particular. Initially psychodynamic causes were considered with the hypothesis that there was a phobic-avoidance response to food resulting from sexual tensions generated by physical changes in puberty. Theories have also included the idea that individual suffering from anorexia fear pregnancy with fantasies of oral impregnation. Starvation is considered a defense. Other theories include the desire to stay in a prepuberty physical state as a way of dealing with sexual anxiety. Other theorists consider the disorder to be genetic or biochemical. The need to be socially accepted and recent fashion trends focusing on the "waif" look have also been considered as influential and a causal factor.

The diagnosis of anorexia is complicated by the fact that a number of other disorders, both physical and psychological, have similar symptoms. These disorders include depression, where weight loss is not uncommon. Other symptoms such as sleep disturbance, obsessive rumination and occasionally suicidal ideation also occur. However, in depressive disorders there is usually not a disturbed body image or fear of weight gain. The depressed individual also often has a decreased appetite. The anorectic does not display loss of appetite until late stage status. Often the anorectic is hyperactive. This is quite different from the agitation sometimes seen in the depressed individual. The person suffering from anorexia displays planned and often ritualistic hyperactivity.

Schizophrenics often display bizarre eating patterns and delusions about food, however they are usually not preoccupied with weight gain fear. Physical and medical problems can cause radical weight loss however in these cases there is not the obsessive component and distorted body image.

The onset of anorexia is often quite sudden and disruptive to the family, especially the parents of an adolescent. As was discussed, adolescents who develop the disorder are often very conscientious and prior to the episode functional. In many cases they are "super achievers" and well liked by peers with a history of social involvement and competency. Changes in behavior often include seclusion, withdrawal, isolation, depression and anhedonia. This behavior is in many cases very sudden and coincides with weight loss and the other symptoms and signs of anorexia.

It is not unusual for the adolescent (or adult) suffering from anorexia to minimize and deny emotional concerns and resist intervention. As was discussed, most weight loss behaviors occur in secret. Often the adolescent has rational excuses for not eating with the family or being absent from the table during meal-times.

Parents tend to be concerned, confused and anxious. Often parents tend to rationalize and minimize themselves. In some cases drug use is suspected (and substance abuse is often coexistent). In other cases significant others focus on external situations and stressors and rationalize that anorexic behaviors are "just a phase." However, with increasing weight loss, emotional and behavioral changes and the development of physical changes and problems, concern becomes more real.

The course of anorexia varies. In some cases there is spontaneous recovery without treatment. In other cases there are periods of remission or partial recovery followed by relapse. Response to treatment varies, however studies indicate a positive response to inpatient treatment. The most consistent indicator of a favorable outcome is early age onset. The indicator for a poor prognosis appears to be late age onset and previous hospitalizations.

A number of treatments have been developed. Recently hospitalization has been utilized. Hospitalization is, of course, required where weight loss is so extreme that death from starvation is possible. Another advantage of hospitalization is controlled eating and isolation from negative stimulation. Stabilization as well as proper diagnosis can be facilitated in a hospital setting. It is important that a psychological assessment be made to identify other concurrent disorders such as depression or personality disorders and to develop a workable treatment plan. As was suggested, eating disorders are psychological in nature and emotional problems must be addressed in treatment.

Many psychiatric hospitals have developed inpatient programs to treat anorexia. Recently intensive outpatient programs have also been developed. These programs are less costly and allow the individual to function and live at home. Outpatient programs, of course, do not provide for as intensive monitoring and control of eating behaviors. Often intensive outpatient treatment is an intermediate form of treatment once the individual has been stabilized and the nutritional state returned to normal. The structure of a hospital program also provides for behavioral management and change therapy although many of the same techniques can be used in outpatient therapy. Both forms of treatment usually include and involve individual, group and family therapy.

Psychotropic drugs have been used in the treatment of eating disorders. Antidepressants are often used. Side effects must be considered as well as the possibility of toxicity due to metabolism problems or electrolyte imbalance.

Family members are impacted by this disorder in a particular way. Eating disorders have a higher rate of mortality than any other psychiatric disorders. Because of this, early and immediate intervention is often necessary. Intervention or treatment is complicated by the tendency to resist treatment as well as a severe form of denial. The individual is not only obsessed with weight loss and fear of weight gain. They usually suffer from a delusional belief system and a distorted view of reality. Reasoning with them about the risks as well as the fact that they are grossly underweight does little good. This is like telling a depressed person not to be depressed or an alcoholic to stop drinking.

Similar to an individual who is addicted to drugs, individuals who suffer from eating disorders have developed a number of defense mechanisms, manipulations and behaviors which allow them to continue the destructive habits and patterns.

The situation is often complicated by the fact that the individual suffering from the disorder is not in contact with significant others on a daily basis. Anorexia often develops in high school with an increase in symptoms on leaving home for school or moving out of the family home to live independently. It is not uncommon for anorectics to secretly engage in eating disorder behaviors for a long period of time without roommates and others identifying or suspecting that they are emotionally ill and suffering from an eating disorder. Because anorexia leads to dehydration, electrolyte imbalance, and malnutrition emergency room admission with fainting, dizziness or even collapse is often one of the first times a significant other, roommate or family member realizes that something is wrong.

Intervention is necessary because eating disorders are chronic and progressive. Long term risks include the possibility of cardiac arrest, cerebral atrophy with irreversible brain damage, stunted physical development and osteoporosis. Because of these risks, plus the risk of death by starvation, family coping techniques such as passive detachment are not recommended. Suggestions include:

1) Recognition of the symptoms and seeking immediate professional help in cases where the symptoms meet the criteria. Most individuals resist treatment and are brought to a physician's office or treatment facility unwilling. Usually the person who brings the individual in for a diagnosis or treatment feels a great deal of guilt and agony.

2) Do not feel guilty. As was discussed, eating disorders, untreated, can result in severe physiological damage. The risks are great.

3) Do not ruminate over the cause of the disorder and internalize blame. It is not uncommon for individuals from functional, loving, supportive families to develop problems. About 8 million people in the U.S. are believed to have this disorder.

4) Emphasize the benefits from treatment. The individual should be reassured that symptoms such as insomnia, depression and obsessive thoughts about food will decrease as well as self-esteem and functional ability improve as the result of treatment.

5) Focus on the individual's emotional and functional well being prior to the onset of the disorder and offer hope and support.

6) Realize that during the initial period of treatment resistance and denial will continue. A "flight to health" with claimed personal insight and promises of more rational behavior is common. Realize that treatment will probably be required for an extensive period of time.

Bulimia nervosa is similar in many ways to anorexia nervosa as far as prevalence, course, treatment and how to deal with the disorder as a family member is concerned. However, there are differences and thus a separate discussion is included on this disorder.

One of the differences is the risk of death. As was discussed, death from starvation is a real threat in the case of anorexia. Anorectics have a disturbance of body image in that they fail to realize the degree of emancipation. (To be diagnosed as anorectic, weight loss or failure to make an expected weight gain during a period of physical development must be 15 percent below normal age/height level.)

The essential features of bulimia are recurrent episodes of binge eating, the feelings of lack of control over eating during binges, regular self induced vomiting, use of laxatives or diuretics, and strict dieting, fasting or exercise to prevent weight gain. The bulimic also is persistently overconcerned about body shape and weight.

Binges are often planned. The food ingested is high in caloric content and usually sweet tasting. Eating is commonly secretive, rapid and continuous until termination by physical discomfort, interruption or sleep. Following a binge, self-hatred and depression is common. Most people with the disorder are within the normal weight range.

The disorder usually begins in adolescent or young adulthood. The disorder tends to be chronic with periods of normal eating. Parents of individuals who suffer from bulimia are often obese. More females than males have the disorder. Obesity in adolescence is a predisposing factor. Bulimia is usually not life threatening however there is danger of electrolyte imbalance, and dehydration which can lead to cardiac problems. Dental erosion and esophageal and gastric problems can also develop. Binge eating is frequently a feature of females with Borderline Personality Disorder.

Bulimia usually begins after a period of dieting. The average length of the binge is about one hour. Most bulimics do not eat regular meals. They prefer to binge at home while alone. The majority of bulimics display some signs of depression. Many have problems with self-concept; have a low self-esteem; are impulsive, compulsive and anxious; and tend to have interpersonal relationship problems. Alcohol abuse is common. Severe weight loss and amenorrhea usually do not occur as they do in anorexia.

Treatment usually is on an outpatient basis with an emphasis on cognitive and behavioral techniques and the development of self-control. A typical program begins with identification of patterns of eating and binging with the development of a self-monitoring system. The individual is encouraged to identify situations and circumstances proceeding loss of control. They are assisted in developing ways to deal with stress. Assertiveness training is often a component. Later in treatment repressed or unconscious unresolved stress related issues and events are explored. Group and individual therapy are also components in treatment. Antidepressant medications may be recommended.

Bulimia often results in feelings of guilt, self-hatred, loss of control and hopelessness. Family members can be supportive and help the individual who is suffering from the disorder by encouraging them to seek treatment and help. This is especially important if there are coexisting problems with alcohol or depression.

Obesity. Family members who live with an individual who is obese have a particular problem. If the obesity is such that the individual's physical health is threatened, of course, there will be concern and attempts to help individuals control their weight and life style habits. Many of the suggestions and recommendations discussed in the chapters covering chemical dependency apply in the case of obesity and eating disorders in the family. Eating disorders have a compulsive obsessive component and nature. Usually the individual suffering from the disorder is in denial and resistant to treatment. Intervention by a professional can often improve reality testing and can be an effective ways of helping the individual enter treatment for the disorder.

Chapter XIII

MAJOR DEPRESSION

Major depression is a type of mood disorder that effects more than 10 million Americans a year. It has been estimated that depression costs the economy over $27 billion a year including $17 billion in time lost on the job. Depression takes a major toll also on family members and significant others.

Depression is one form of mood disorder. The other form is bipolar disorder which will be discussed in the next chapter. Bipolar disorder is characterized by at least one episode of manic mood elevation or hypomanic elevation. A depressive disorder does not have this period of mood elevation. During the depressive episode, mood is depressed with loss of interest as well as several associated features such as weight loss and difficulty with concentration. There are two types of depressive disorders. One, which we will focus on, is major depression. The other is dysthymia. *DSM IV* also lists a residual category called Depressive Disorder, Not Otherwise Specified which is a category for forms of depression which do not meet the criteria for major depression and dysthymia. Dysthymia, generally is a form of depression which is not as pervasive and debilitating as major depression.

Major depression is more than a state of sadness or melancholia. It is also more than an adjustment to an identifiable stressor such as death in the family or a divorce although such an event can and often does precede and or precipitate a depressive episode.

In order for a disorder to be classified as a major depression there must be at least one major depressive episode. The criteria for a major depressive episode is either a depressed mood or loss of interest which is a change from the previous level of functioning. Other symptoms include difficulty in concentration; anhedonia; chronic fatigue; decreased effectiveness or productivity at work, home or school; feelings of hopelessness, helplessness or low self-esteem; disturbed appetite and or sleeping; a negative attitude and outlook on life; tearfulness; decreased sexual interest and thoughts of death and suicide.

Major depression may be mild with few of the above mentioned symptoms, moderate or severe. There may be psychotic features such as delusions or not. Psychotic features, when present, may be related to the depression such as delusions of inadequacy, guilt, disease, death and deserved punishment or non-mood congruent with themes such as persecution. Major depression may recur. It may be in partial remission or full remission. The disorder may be chronic which means that the episode has lasted for more than two consecutive years or acute. In order to be classified as major depression the episode must have lasted for at least two weeks.

The individual suffering from major depression may deny feeling depressed or may not complain of loss of interest or pleasure however family members will usually notice withdrawal and an attitude of disinterest. While weight loss is common, individuals who are suffering from major depression may also increase food consumption. Sufferers usually complain of insomnia; however in some instances there is a tendency to over-sleep. Depressed people tend to be agitated. Problems with sitting, pacing and handwringing are not uncommon. On the other hand there may be a decrease in energy level. Reasoning, judgement and problem solving abilities are often impaired by a mood disorder. Individuals who are depressed are often indecisive. Decisions on the job and in everyday living become difficult and are often postponed. In many cases there are related physical complaints including headaches, backaches, nausea and constipation. A preoccupation with death is common as well as suicide. Research has indicated that risk of suicide increases as the individual gains energy. In the early stage of depression individuals often are incapacitated. However, as the depression continues there often develops a feeling of hopelessness and despair. Previous suicide attempts, of course, add to concern about the possibility of suicide during a current episode. Individuals with a plan are also more at risk for suicide. Depressed individuals who use alcohol and other mood altering drugs are also at risk. Suicidal thoughts should always be taken seriously. There has been a significant increase in teenage suicides in the last ten years. Parents and significant others should be aware of this and seek immediate professional help in the case of a family member who talks about or threatens suicide.

Major depression affects children, adolescents and adults. We in the mental health field are observing more children who are depressed. Common symptoms in children who are suffering from depression are somatic complaints and agitation. Frequently there are also auditory hallucinations such as a voice talking to the child. Adolescents present differently. Commonly they are either negative or antisocial or both. Adolescents tend to act out their depression more so than children. School performance problems, legal infractions, gang membership, drug use, oppositional and defiant behavior at home and in school, lack of motivation and effort, and irritability are other signs of adolescent depression. Adolescents who are experiencing depression often express boredom and the desire to leave home. Commonly they are sullen, non-verbal (or argumentative), and angry. They resist involvement in family activities and often refuse to disclose and discuss their feelings and reasons for their behaviors.

Parents often relate these attitudes and behaviors to "growing up". Indeed, there are physical, social and life stage problems and stresses on adolescents preparing to enter young adulthood. Developmentally they are dealing with establishing their own sense of identity as well as their own value system. Adolescents are very sensitive to the opinions of others. They tend to focus on their own problems and concerns and often have little awareness of how their behaviors impact on others. The drive for autonomy, independence and separation often takes the form of rebellion and rejection of family. However, life stage factors and social developmental issues normally do not result in major depression. Certainly there will be mood changes and mood swings; however the parent or significant other who notes major depression symptoms should be concerned.

Life stage factors as well as characterological factors and psychosocial stressors can precipitate depression in adults. At this time it should be noted that major depression can be endogenous, exogenous or a combination of both. Endogenous depression is related to a chemical imbalance in the brain. Medication coupled with therapy can often restore balance. Characterological factors also effect the way people respond to life and life stressors. Some individuals tend to be negative and pessimistic. Others are overly optimistic. Personality disorders can and often do coexist with mood disorders.

Life stage psychology is the study of social and psychological factors which effect human behavior. Theorists have identified various stages of life, each with its own stressors and tasks to be completed. Entering these stages and going from one developmental level often creates stress and dysphoria. For example, entering young adulthood is stressful not only as related to leaving home but as far as providing for oneself. Entering adulthood has been postponed by society. The rituals have also changed. A generation ago young people commonly completed their education, entered the work force, married and began raising a family. They entered the "settling in" stage. Today, young people often postpone these commitments. It is not uncommon to find someone in their late 20's and early 30's who is still struggling with issues of identity, career choice and value formulation.

Middle age stage adults also have pressures and stresses which may not have been present a few decades ago. One of them is not only caring and providing for their own family (sometimes to include young adult children) but also for aging parents. Plans for their own security and retirement are often tempered by financial obligations to other family members. Middle aged adults often also experience midlife crisis. Pop psychology has over used this term however there is research to document a time of appraisal of accomplishments and personal progress which takes place in midlife. Often this appraisal results in improved reality testing but feelings of failure and personal disappointment. Recent economic trends toward downsizing have added to insecurity in middle age as well as employment concerns among this age group.

What was previously known as "old age" is now broken down into three basic categories. These might be called the "go go" age where individuals commonly in retirement from 65 to 75 live independent, vital lives. "Slow go" from 70 or so to 80–85 where physical conditions may require some form of outside help, and "no go" in which case more intensive care is required. Of course, as in all stages of life, there are a great deal of individual differences related to characterological factors, health, financial situation and emotional and psychological condition. Aging can result in depression. As was discussed in the chapter on Alzheimer's, many elderly people who are diagnosed as demented are actually depressed and can be treated successfully for depression.

Major depression can develop over a period of days or a few weeks or it may be sudden, especially in the case of a severe psychosocial stressor such as job loss or death. (Again major depression is different from normal bereavement.) Depression can also be seasonal or non-seasonal. Hospitalization due to depression tends to increase during periods of decreased daylight.

Untreated episodes of depression tend to last six months or longer. In most cases there is remission and return to the previous level of functioning; however in a number of cases some symptoms last longer. Level of impairment (and the degree of impact on family members) varies from individual to individual; however in order to be classified as major depression there must be some impairment in functioning. Impairment can be so severe that the individual is unable to care for self. Also, of course, there can be the risk of self-destruction.

Chronic physical illness, legal or financial problems, death of a loved one, divorce and sometimes childbirth can precipitate an episode. In cases of endogenous depression identifiable psychosocial stressor may or may not be present as well as in the case of seasonal depression.

Depression in a family impacts the various members differently just as the severity, chronicity and type depression has a different impact. Children in a family in which one of the parents is suffering from major depression often complain of emotional problems and display symptoms of stress. In some cases the depressed parent's emotional state and problems result in the spouse focusing on that individual. Often children resent the lack of attention and feel abused, abandoned and uncared for during childhood. These feelings can result in insecurity, anger and resentment in later life. In situations where the parent has been hospitalized because of depression there may be anxiety and confusion. (Hospitalization is often recommended where there is risk of suicide, pervasive dysfunctional impairment without response to outpatient therapy and medication, or to provide intensive treatment to hasten improvement.) Children also commonly feel guilty. In many family systems there are responses similar to those of systems in which a parent is chemically dependent. Children are taught to keep their problems and their feelings to themselves. Roles similar to those discussed in previous chapters tend to develop. Frequently there is acting out.

The spouse of an individual who suffers from major depression is also in a particular situation. If the depression is severe there often develops financial problems. In many cases there is anticipatory anxiety that an episode will occur. There are often feelings of hopelessness, helplessness and powerlessness as well as anguish and feelings of sadness, empathy and compassion. In many cases the depression has not been adequately diagnosed and treated and the mood swings and behaviors are considered controllable. Marital conflict and discord often result, sometimes with divorce or separation the outcome. Relationships are complicated if the individual uses alcohol or other mood altering drugs to self-medicate. (This should not be confused with antidepressant medication use under the care of a physician. Antidepressant drugs are not addictive and have been used with significant positive benefit, especially combined with psychotherapy to improve adaptive functional and interpersonal abilities and to deal with related emotional issues.)

There is the danger of the spouse becoming a codependent or an enabler. Often the significant other/spouse develops symptoms of depression and or anxiety. Mood swings on the part of the individual diagnosed as depressed produce a reactionary change in mood in the significant other. Feelings of anger, resentment, abuse and despair are not uncommon.

Dealing with an elderly parent who is depressed also creates particular problems and feelings. Adult children often have responsibilities and lives of their own which makes care and special attention difficult. In situations where the adult child is responsible for primary care, there can be feelings of anger as well as frustration. Reversal of the child parent role creates dysphoria. Fortunately society and the community have become more aware of the needs of the elderly and treatment of geriatric depression has become more available. Medication must be administered on the basis of the special needs of the elderly as well as considerations including decrease in metabolism and synergetic effects of other medications. There is the risk of overmedication or medication merely to control behavior. As was discussed, a neuropsychological or psychological assessment is recommended in situations where dementia is suspected, and when there are symptoms of emotional and psychological distress.

Parents of children and adolescents suffering from major depression also experience particular emotions and stress. Childhood/adolescent depression is often not expected or anticipated. Development of the symptoms and behaviors can be very sudden. Because adolescents often do not know how to express their feelings or are unaware of their feelings, parents are frequently "the last to know." Parents can become confused, anxious and sometimes angry. Antisocial and rebellious behaviors, often uncharacteristic in the past, create family stress, disruption and conflict. Siblings tend to become anxious and confused. Marital conflict can develop based on previously unresolved stress and disagreement or on differences in how to deal with the family crisis.

Many of the suggestions and recommendations discussed previously in relationship to dealing with mental illness in the family apply in cases of major depression. When the symptoms of major depression are observed and the disorder suspected, it is primary that the family member get professional help. Treatment progress has been made using a combination of medication and psychotherapy. Hospitalization is usually not required and a last resort. However, there is no need for the individual and the family to suffer over a long period of time while the disorder becomes progressively worse or the behavioral, functional relationship problems increase.

Specific suggestions, based on relationship to the individual with the disorder, include:

1) Children of a depressed parent. Children need to understand what is taking place and to be assured that their security and dependency needs are met. They may need special love and attention. The parents must be honest and open. In cases where the "sick" parent is hospitalized suddenly and returns later with no explanation, the child tends to be confused and often traumatized. The parent who has the disorder should discuss his or her feelings with the family. Often the parent feels guilty and angry. These feelings should be explored in therapy; however the family is entitled to know what the person feels and usually will be very supportive. Children and adolescents who grow up in a family where one parent suffers from depression may also benefit from individual therapy to ventilate their feelings, discuss fears that they too might develop the disorder and to educate themselves.

2) Spouses must be sure that they do not become enablers and codependents. They may want to participate in individual therapy to help them cope as well as ventilate their feelings. Marital therapy might be appropriate. Self-help groups are available for family members of individuals with mental disorders. Remember, mental disorders and problems are common, just as physical and medical problems are. Don't be judgemental and try not to be guilty and angry.

3) Adult children of depressed parents often experience problems related to unresolved childhood issues. This can create problems in the present relationship, when the parent is suffering from depression. Threats and fears of suicide can also create anxiety and dysphoria.

4) Parents of children and adolescents who are suffering from depression must realize that they have not, directly, caused the depression. They must be available and realize that this is a time when the

child or adolescent needs support and assurance that they are loved and will be cared for in the future. Children and adolescents suffering from depression usually have a great fear of never returning to a stage of happiness and normalcy. Understand this and discuss choices for treatment focusing primarily on the fact that there are problems and that there is professional help to solve these problems. Help the child or adolescent choose a therapist or counselor who understands children and adolescents. It is primary that a therapeutic relationship and commitment be developed. Therapy is a team process and most successful when the individual in treatment is respected and not belittled. Issues of authority and control must not be allowed to develop when working with an adolescent. A practical, pragmatic approach is recommended focusing on helping the individual identify problems and concerns and developing more adequate and adaptive problem solving skills and abilities. This is called Reality Therapy. Before choosing a psychologist or therapist to work with the adolescent and family discuss the individual's experience, training and approach.

Chapter XIV

BIPOLAR DISORDER (MANIC-DEPRESSION)

The second type of mood disorder is bipolar disorder commonly known as manic depression because, all forms of this disorder include a manic or hypomanic episode. Bipolar I Disorders include manic episodes. Bipolar II disorders include a hypomanic episode without a manic episode. Hypomanic episodes are less severe than manic episodes. Bipolar I disorders are especially disruptive to significant others and family members because of the nature of manic episodes.

A manic episode is a period of abnormal elevated mood. During this period the sufferer displays a number of the following symptoms:

1) Grandiosity or inflated self-esteem.
2) Hypersomnia with a decrease in the need for sleep.
3) Hyperverbalization or pressured speech.
4) Mind racing and flight of ideas. Often there is tangential thought processes.
5) Poor attention and inability to stay focused with a tendency to be preoccupied with insignificant or irrelevant external stimuli.
6) Compulsiveness.
7) And involvement in activities which have a potential for painful consequences such as buying sprees, gambling, sexual promiscuity and poor financial investments.

This disorder is disturbing to family members not only because judgement, reasoning and reality testing are impaired but also because of the risk that the individual will act in such a way as to jeopardize the financial position of the family or injure himself or herself, or others. Individuals who are experiencing a manic episode usually cannot be reasoned with. Their behaviors make sense to them because these behaviors are based on psychotic and delusional thinking. Money is often withdrawn from savings for an irrational reason. It is not unusual for individuals who are manic to buy cars, boats, or other types of material goods on whim and impulse. A tendency to be grandiose and irritable adds to family problems. The fact that episodes are often sudden and unrelated to an obvious stressor creates an added element of anxiety, fear and concern in the family.

Mania can be classified as mild, moderate or severe. Psychotic features such as delusions and hallucinations are possible. The themes of these psychotic features include inflated sense of self-worth, power, special knowledge and often a special relationship to a diety or famous person. Delusions may also be persecutory or paranoid. In cases where delusions are present, there is an increase of risk as well as increased irrationality and lack of reality testing. Individuals who suffer from paranoid delusions can become violent and aggressive. Attempts to reason with a person experiencing a manic or hypomanic episode are often ineffective. These attempts often elicit exacerbated symptoms and acting out.

In all cases of Bipolar I disorder there is evidence of a manic episode. If the current episode involves intermixed or rapidly alternating manic and depressive episodes the disorder is classified as "mixed." In situations where the symptoms do not include depression the bipolar disorder is classified as "manic." Bipolar Disorder, depressed is used to describe a condition where the individual has experienced a manic episode in the past, however is currently displaying symptoms of major depression.

Usually the individual who is bipolar does not realize that they are ill and resists any attempts for treatment. Radical mood changes and episodes of anger and threats of assault are not uncommon and make management by the family difficult if not impossible. Often family members attempt to control or manage the individual at home, especially during the early year or years of the development of the disorder. This is due in part to failure to understand the nature of the disorder. Family members often look for the cause of the episode and on occasion blame drug use for the irrational, manic responses. Just as in other mental disorders in the family there is often confusion, shock and denial.

Studies suggest that age of onset is usually in the early 20's although symptoms can appear after age 50. Manic episodes usually begin suddenly. Symptoms tend to become more extreme over the course of the episode. Episodes may last from a few days to months without treatment and often end abruptly. Impairment can be severe. Financial loss and legal problems are not uncommon. Often stressors precipitate an episode; however in other cases there is no identifiable situation or psychosocial stressor. Research has suggested that antidepressant medication can cause a manic episode. This is one reason that an accurate diagnosis is primary. In situations of bipolar disorder, depressed it is not uncommon for a physician to prescribe an antidepressant. Family members or significant others must be very specific in describing past behaviors and, if past manic episodes have been observed when informing the psychiatrist.

Around 1 percent of all adults suffer from bipolar disorder. Usually a manic episode is the precipitator for hospitalization. The disorder is found in an equal number among males and females. There appears to be a genetic disposition for bipolar disorder in families. This has resulted in the hypothesis that the disorder is one of chemical imbalance. Treatment has been successful using a combination of drugs and psychotherapy. Psychotherapy is suggested for a number of reasons. One of the primary reasons is to explain the nature of the disorder and help the individual who is suffering from the illness to accept the fact that he or she is ill and probably will have to take medication for an extended period of time, possibly life time.

Acceptance of these facts (first that one suffers from a mental disorder and secondly that medication will be required) is difficult especially for a young adult with the disorder. As in most cases of illness, facts and reality are often denied. Young adults frequently experience feelings of narcissistic injury and become emotionally distraught. They often feel that they are "different" and defective. Commonly there are feelings of anger, confusion, hopelessness and helplessness.

Many individuals who are bipolar hope for an immediate and complete "cure." Medication may be taken for a short period of time; however individuals with bipolar disorder often complain of the side effects and frequently stop taking medication because they "like" being hypomanic and energized. It is not uncommon for the therapist to have to monitor medical compliance and continually reinforce the need for medication. Just as many individuals who are chemically dependent tend to rationalize that indeed they can "control" use (after a period of abstinence), sufferers of bipolar disorder tend to intellectualize and deny. There is a tendency to want to believe that they have "outgrown" the disorder and that episodes will not recur.

While medication tends to stabilize mood, side effects are possible and often disturbing and annoying. These side effects include vomiting, diarrhea, tremors, drowsiness, poor coordination, staggering, confusion or twitching. Lithium Carbonate (the most commonly used medication) can also cause drowsiness. Side effects commonly decrease following the initial period of use. Pregnant women and nursing mothers and individuals with heart or kidney disease should not be prescribed Lithium. There is some concern that the medication over a long period of time might cause thyroid and or renal problems. Intermittent use is often recommended which, of course, increases the risk of recurrent pathology. Thus, the patient and family are confronted with a dilemma.

Because of these side effects and a tendency for lack of treatment compliance, it is important for a therapeutic relationship to be established with a professional who is familiar with the disorder and a specialist. A team of specialists might be considered with a physician focusing on the biochemical aspect of the disorder, and monitoring of the Lithium blood level as well as possible related medical problems, and a psychologist or other type of therapist being concerned with the emotional and behavioral aspects of the disorder.

As was suggested, often failure to recognize and treat the disorder has resulted in severely conflicted relationships and emotional problems that are secondary to the disorder. The individual who is afflicted often feels angry, depressed and hopeless. Family members are often angry, confused and depressed.

Specific suggestions in dealing with the disorder in the family include:

1) Overcoming denial and helping the individual realize that professional help is needed. Hospitalization might be necessary, especially when the episode is severe. This not only results in stabilization but provides an opportunity for an accurate diagnosis and the development of a treatment plan.

2) Discuss with the individual and other family members your fears, concerns and anxiety. It is important that all significant others and family members become aware of the nature of the disorder.

3) Make plans for the future and possible actions which can be taken in the case of a recurrent episode. Often the individual who is suffering from the disorder can, over time, recognize symptoms and seek help. Communication must be open so that you as a significant other can be available and reinforce the disclosure of early symptoms for treatment and management. Often the individual feels shame, guilt and fear and attempts to hide symptoms. This creates anxiety and tension and can precipitate an episode. A caring, supportive, understanding spouse, family member or significant other can provide stability.

4) Be practical and direct. It might be of benefit to take steps to decrease the possibility of financial ruin or family legal problems by talking with an attorney. A discussion such as this should include the individual with the disorder. During periods between episodes the individual with the disorder is usually rational and as concerned about the impact of episodes on the family situation as are significant others and the family themselves.

5) Bipolar disorder can usually be treated with a combination of medication and therapy. Realize this and continue your life. Individual therapy might be of benefit. Learning about the disorder is primary. There are support groups for individuals who suffer from bipolar disorder as well as self-help groups for family members.

Chapter XV

INTERMITTENT EXPLOSIVE DISORDER

(Rage Episode Disorder and Spouse Abuse)

Intermittent explosive disorder is a form of impulse control disorder as are the chemical abuse and dependence disorders and the sexual disorders. A chapter has been included on this disorder because of the traumatic impact of this illness on the family.

Intermittent explosive disorder (IED) requires that there be several discrete episodes of loss of control resulting in serious destruction of property or assault to others. The degree of aggressiveness must be significantly out of proportion to the circumstances. In order to be classed as IED the response must not be the result of intoxication or organic problems. It is not uncommon for individuals who are intoxicated or using other drugs (especially hallucinogens) to act aggressively. In cases of IED the aggressive assaultive behavior takes place without provocations during a period of sobriety.

This disorder is considered rare. The disorder is more common among males than females. The first symptoms of the disorder usually appear in the 20's or 30's although it can begin at any time of life. The unpredictable nature of the disorder as well as the possibility of assault and damage to property results in anxiety in the family. Often, one particular member of the family is the object of the assault however this is not always the case.

The person who has these episodes often describes them as "spells or attacks." There is usually a sudden onset and a sudden remission. Frequently remorse and guilt are expressed following an episode. There has been speculation that this disorder is the result of a chemical imbalance or brain disorder. Medication has been used to treat the disorder; however very little research has been completed regarding treatment response, course and cause. There appears to be a familial pattern.

Some studies have found that during the episode or following the episode there is an alternation in sensorium including a sense of disorientation. Individuals who experience this disorder often report that they were unaware of their surroundings and their behaviors. Hypersensitivity has also been reported as well as hyperactivity and restlessness and agitation prior to an episode. Nonspecific electroencephalogram findings and soft neurological signs have also been observed. (Of course, testing during an episode is almost impossible.)

Anticonvulsants have been used in treatment as well as Lithium. Previously, neurosurgical intervention was used in an attempt to treat IED however this is no longer considered appropriate. Psychotherapy is often suggested in tandem with medication to deal with the trauma and anxiety in the family created by the rage episodes. Treatment is often resisted.

IED is considered, along with rage episodes related to alcohol and drug abuse, as a major causal factor in spouse abuse. It is estimated that between three and six million families experience spouse abuse each year. Many of these cases are not reported. Most of the situations involve the wife being abused by the husband, however, there appear to be a number of cases of husband abuse, especially where the husband is an elderly frail man married to a younger woman. While this discussion will focus primarily on physical assault and abuse, of course, emotional abuse can also be devastating and traumatic. Wife beating occurs in all socioeconomic levels and categories. Violence in the family is not always condemned. A recent national study of adult men and women reported that 20 percent of the sample approved of a husband hitting a wife. Up until 1874 the law permitted such action in the U.S. Even today prosecution of wife beaters is rare. Society appears to blame the woman. Leaving home is often difficult for the wife not only because of financial problems and family obligations but also because of social norms.

Abusive men are likely to come from abusive homes. The individuals tend to be immature, dependent and suffer from feelings of impotence and inadequacy. Once the initial episode takes place, the abuse usually continues. Episodes can be precipitated by psychosocial stressors such as financial or work problems. Individuals who abuse a spouse take out their feelings of frustration and anger on the spouse rather than dealing with the problems facing them. Studies have suggested that abusiveness often increases when the wife is least available such as during pregnancy or when she has small children. Often an abusive husband restricts a wife's social involvement and career. He tends to be jealous and possessive. Working outside of the home causes fear for the husband not only because external social relationships are formed but because of fear of abandonment.

Women in abusive relationships tend to come from violent homes also. They commonly marry at an early age. Abusive husbands usually do not abuse the wife until after the marriage. Feelings of dependency and acceptance of the male role of dominance, plus the wife's typical feelings of inadequacy, often results in women returning to abusive spouses. Feelings of vulnerability and fear of social criticism prevents disclosure to family, friends or authorities. Even following disclosure, help is not readily available in many cases. Mental health professionals, police and ministers too often resist involvement.

Fortunately hot lines and shelters have recently been established, although frequently wives take action only when one of their children has been threatened or abused. (As was discussed, rage episodes can involve any and or all the members of a family.)

Therapy is based on the fact that the abuse will change only when the abused spouse demonstrates that he or she will not tolerate the abuse. One intervention is for the spouse to leave with the condition of return based on therapy for the abuser. Unfortunately most abusers will not enter therapy.

Abused spouses often need therapy not only to cope with current problems, but feelings of failure, guilt, anger and depression. Unresolved issues regarding dependency, fear of rejection and abandonment, low self-esteem and lack of identity must also be addressed. Healing the pain will take time. Abused spouses often display symptoms of post traumatic stress disorder. Medication (to deal with depression) as well as psychotherapy is often recommended.

Suggestions for the abused spouse include:

1) Improve reality testing. Evaluate the situation and the prognosis for change.
2) Protect yourself and your family. This often means leaving home with the children.
3) Seek professional help for yourself and family including legal advice. Often the children will need to become involved in therapy.
4) Do not give up hope. You are a valuable, unique, special person entitled to personal growth, happiness and fulfillment. Do not continue to live in fear, anxiety and despair.

Chapter XVI

PATHOLOGICAL GAMBLING

Pathological gambling is another mental disorder that tends to have severe impact on the family and the family life style. Like addictive disorders, pathological gambling is an impulse control disorder. Like alcoholism and spouse abuse, there is often remorse following episodes and endless promises of change. Family members impacted by pathological gambling tend to report feelings of hopelessness and emotional exhaustion due to broken promises, increasing financial problems, and lack of honesty and deceit. Pathological gamblers, like chemically addicted individuals, tend to have developed very clever ways of manipulating others in order to continue their addictive habits and behaviors. They also have a tendency to resist treatment. Family members commonly are angry, frustrated, depressed and anxious. One of the common defense mechanisms used by family members is withdrawal. This, of course, results in unmet relationship needs and in many cases an empty marriage in the situation where the family gambler is a spouse. Children tend to develop many of the personality traits, attitudes and behaviors often found among children who grow up in a dysfunctional family including anxiety, lack of trust in others, problems with intimacy and problems with emotional awareness.

The individual who is a pathological gambler tends to be preoccupied with gambling and focuses attention on getting money in order to gamble. The amount of money gambled and the frequency is greater than intended reflecting loss of control. Restlessness results when prevented from gambling. The individual tends to gamble as a way of escaping problems. Amounts gambled tend to increase. Lying is common to conceal losses. Illegal acts to finance gambling are also common.

Attempting to win back losses is common as are repeated failed efforts to stop. Gambling interferes with normal and expected social, career and recreational activities. The individual continues to gamble although the resulting problems are known. Stress tends to increase the urge to gamble.

(Thus codependents tend to try to reduce stress for the gambler.) Legal problems resulting from unpaid debts are common.

Pathological gamblers tend to be preoccupied with money as the solution to their problems. Reality testing is faulty. They usually ignore solutions to their problems which require extra effort or personal commitment. Antisocial behaviors to support their compulsive habit such as stealing from an employer are not uncommon. Gambling appears to be related to the need for importance, power and excitement. Some theorists have speculated that the underlying cause for the disorder is either characterological or endogenous depression. The disorder usually begins in adolescence with males. Females develop the disorder later. The disorder tends to be chronic although there are sometimes periods of remission. Pathological gambling like most of the sexual impulse disorders is difficult to treat. The prognosis is usually guarded. Drug abuse and dependence, depression with suicidal ideations and/or gestures, legal problems, and family conflict are associated features. This disorder affects between 2 percent and 3 percent of the adult population. There are more male pathological gamblers than females.

Pathological gambling appears to be a conditioned response more than genetic and is probably related to emotional, social and cognitive factors. Research has suggested that certain situations and factors are predisposing including inappropriate discipline in childhood (too harsh, inconsistent or too lenient) a family of origin that was preoccupied with material success or wealth; loss of a parent or divorce or separation of parents; and exposure to gambling at an early age. Some theorists have speculated that pathological gamblers have an unconscious desire to lose and for punishment.

Medication has been used in treatment as well as psychotherapy. Family involvement is suggested as a form of intervention and a way to deal with feelings resulting from the behavior of the gambler. Gamblers Anonymous (GA) is a self-help group.

The previous chapters have offered suggestions for coping with mental illness in the family in general as well as impulse control disorders specifically. It might be of benefit to reread these chapters, especially Chapter VII and VIII on alcoholism. Many of the principles and techniques apply. Other suggestions include:

1) Realization that pathological gambling is usually chronic.
2) Focus on your own needs, goals and situation.

3) Take precautions to protect and provide for yourself and your family.
4) Decide which behaviors you are willing to accept and live with and set limits and boundaries. Do not enable.
5) Individual therapy might be of benefit.
6) And, remember you did not cause the family member to become a pathological gambler and you cannot cure it. Encourage him or her to get treatment and go on with your life. Good luck.

Chapter XVII

SEXUAL DISORDERS—PARAPHILIAS

Exhibitionism, Fetishism, Frotteurism, Pedophilia, Masochism, Sadism, Voyeurism, and Transvestism

There are two categories of sexual disorders—paraphilias and sexual dysfunction. This chapter will focus on paraphilias. Paraphilias are defined as abnormal arousal to objects and situations with a resulting interference in the ability to participate in a reciprocal, affectionate activity. The primary feature of these disorders is an intense recurrent sexual urge and arousing fantasies involving nonhuman objects, non-consenting persons or the experiencing of humiliation of oneself or humiliating one's partner. In order for the diagnosis to be made the individual suffering from this disorder has acted on these urges or is distressed by them. In the past these disorders have been referred to as sexual deviations.

These disorders tend to be chronic and difficult to treat. Often there is a great feeling of shame and attempts to hide these behaviors and urges. These disorders are commonly devastating to family members who often feel used, guilty, responsible, angry, repulsed or confused.

In some cases the paraphilia is acted out with a consenting partner. However, usually it is not shared by a partner. In extreme cases it is acted out with a nonconsenting partner. Treatment of these disorders is usually not sought with an individual coming into treatment primarily under pressure from society (in the case of illegal acts) or a significant other.

Concurrent disorders should be addressed in treatment as well as the sexual disorder. Acting out the urge or fantasy tends to increase with stress. Individuals with these disorders tend to choose situations and occupations that expose them to possible stimulation. For example, pedophilics tend to work with children. In many cases the person with the disorder does not suffer remorse or distress. However, others report extreme shame and depression. Impairment varies depending on the degree of severity of the disorder and the type. However, in all cases the ability to have mutually satisfying affectionate sex with another is affected.

Complications include the risk of physical injury in sexual masochism, and possible arrest and prosecution in paraphilias such as voyeurism, exhibitionism, pedophilia, frotteurism and sadism. Paraphillic behavior tends to be recurrent, resulting in the speculation that a number of people have been victimized. The availability of paraphillic pornography and paraphernalia supports the hypothesis that these disorders are more prevalent than treatment figures would suggest.

Severity ranges from mild where the urges cause significant distress but have never been acted on, to severe where the urges are acted on repeatedly.

Exhibitionism is defined as an intense, recurrent urge and/or fantasy to expose one's genitals to an unsuspecting stranger. As in all paraphilias, the individual suffering from the disorder must experience either marked distress or have acted on the urge over the last six months. If the person acts on the urge, there is no attempt for further sexual activity with the victim; however, masturbation does often occur. The disorder usually begins before age 18. There tend to be few exhibitionists over age 40.

Fetishism is sexual arousal involving nonliving objects such as female undergarments. Cross dressing and use of a device for tactile genital stimulation is not included in the category of objects. Masturbation usually occurs during the period of arousal. Sexual partners may be asked to wear particular objects during this time. Absence of the object often results in erectile inability in males. Onset is common during adolescence. Like most paraphilias, the disorder is usually chronic.

Frotteurism also usually begins during adolescence; however it tends to decline in frequency after age 25. The disorder is defined as the urge or fantasy to touch or rub against an unconsenting person. This does not include sexual arousal with a consenting sexual partner. The offense usually takes place in a crowded public place.

Pedophilia involves sexual activity with a prepubescent child or children usually under the age of 13. The offender must be at least 16 and at least 5 years older than the victim. The relationship can be same sex, opposite sex or same and opposite sex. It is also classified as incestual or nonincestual and exclusively children or non-exclusive type.

The attraction is usually for a particular age range within a year or two. The type of sexual activity varies; however, it is always intrusive. Because the perpetrator is older, there is always an element of power, intimidation or authority. Age at onset is usually adolescence with the course of the disorder chronic. Stress often precipitates acting on the urges. Individuals with same sex attraction appear to be less responsive to treatment. Treatment is seldom voluntary and usually court ordered. The following chapter will discuss childhood sexual abuse—symptoms to look for, impact, and treatment approaches.

Sexual masochism is the recurrent intense urge or fantasy involving being humiliated, beaten, bound or made to suffer. This must be real, not simulated. Fantasies often involve being raped without possibility of escape. In some cases individuals bind themselves or self-mutilate. In other cases a partner is used to act out the urge. Hypoxyphilia is especially dangerous and involves sexual arousal by being deprived of oxygen. Other forms of masochism involve spanking, whipping, electric shocks, cutting and piercing, burning, being urinated on, defecated on, being subjected to verbal abuse or commanded to perform humiliating acts.

This disorder is suspected to have its onset during childhood. Acting out these urges commonly takes place by early adulthood. This disorder is difficult to treat with a tendency for continuation of the behaviors and urges. The severity of the acts may increase over time or during periods of stress with an increase in the risk for injury and death.

Sexual sadism involves acts in which the psychological or physical suffering of the victim causes sexual arousal. These acts may take place with a consenting partner. In other cases there is a victim. Usually the severity of the acts increases over time with a concurrent increase in risk to the involved sexual partner or victim. The suffering of the victim is what causes the sexual arousal. These acts must be real, not simulated. Individuals who suffer from antisocial personality disorder as well as sexual sadism are potentially very dangerous.

Transvestic fetishism involves the urge or fantasy to cross dress. This urge must have been acted on during the past six months or the urge or fantasy must cause marked distress. Normally in the early stages of the disorder, the urge is resisted with related anxiety and distress. Once the urge is acted on there appears to be a pattern of recurrent acting out. Masturbation usually takes place with the individual having fantasies of being attractive to other males while dressed in female clothes. The diagnosis is used where there is no gender disorder such as transexualism in which the individual has a desire to acquire the sexual characteristic of the opposite sex, although there may be gender dysphoria and gender role or identity discomfort.

The degree of cross dressing varies. In some cases one article of opposite sex apparel may be worn. In others the individual may dress entirely in opposite sex clothing and wear make up. It is interesting that the diagnosis and all research focuses on males who cross dress for sexual arousal. Little has been written about the possibility of females (without gender identity disturbance) who may cross dress as males for sexual stimulation and arousal.

The disorder usually begins in childhood or adolescence. There has been some suggestion that transvestic fetishism is related to the early childhood experience of humiliating a boy by dressing him in female clothes.

Voyeurism involves sexual stimulation from watching unsuspecting people who are naked in the process of undressing or involved in sexual activity. Masturbation usually takes place with no desire to have sexual activity with the person observed. This disorder usually begins in early puberty and the course tends to be chronic.

Treatment of the paraphilias is difficult because the repetitive nature of the disorder tends to reinforce the disorder itself. In other words, the individual tends to eliminate other choices and methods of sexual stimulation with arousal becoming more and more entrenched and the individual is more dependent on paraphillic fantasies and behaviors for satisfaction. Some positive results have been reported using antiandrogens in treatment. However, relapse and recidivism is significant. The degree of compulsion tends to decrease with age. This is probably related to a decrease in sexual drive. There are also instances of intermittency with recurrence under stress. Spontaneous recovery is very unusual.

Of course, family members are impacted in different ways not only by their relationship to the individual who is paraphillic but also as related to the particular type and severity of the disorder. Because the paraphilia behaviors are often secretive, lack of knowledge is not uncommon. Once the behavior becomes suspected or known, relationships of course are affected. Children and adolescents are usually confused, angry and upset when a parent is discovered to be acting in an abnormal way or have abnormal fantasies and urges.

The spouse in the case of the secret paraphilia commonly feels betrayed. In cases where secretiveness is not an issue there is often the feeling of not being adequate. Spouses may blame themselves as not being sexually desirable or adequate.

In situations where the disorder is severe, interpersonal relationship, social involvement and work activities may be impaired with a preoccupation with the paraphilia. Arrest and prosecution of course not only creates financial problems but also emotional trauma for the offender as well as for all family members.

The type and severity of the disorder determines the impact on family members. In some cases there may be a capacity for affection and a relationship. In other cases behaviors become almost psychotic or neurotic with the compulsive and obsessive components precluding a healthy relationship.

Family members, especially adults and spouses, must make decisions for their own benefit and need satisfaction based not only on the prognosis for treatment and change, but their own feelings regarding the behaviors of the significant other or family member. These decisions might involve the help of a professional. Often shock, guilt, shame and confusion impair judgement and reasoning. Of course, in cases of incest, the children must be protected.

Chapter XVIII

CHILDHOOD SEXUAL ABUSE

Symptoms, Impact and Treatment Approaches

Research has indicated that certain events, factors, and experiences tend to predispose an individual for emotional problems. These may be genetic, situational, or environmental. For example, there is evidence to support the hypothesis that there is a genetic factor related to schizophrenia, endogenous depression and possible chemical dependency.

Individuals who grow up in a dysfunctional family, children of divorce, and children who are adopted tend to experience emotional problems at a higher rate than the general population. This chapter on childhood sexual abuse is included because the impact of this experience often appears to be traumatic and to affect functional ability and emotional stability in later years. Therapists have often found symptoms of Post Traumatic Stress Disorder (PTSD) and in some cases use PTSD intervention techniques to treat individuals who have experienced sexual abuse as children. Physical and verbal abuse during childhood also can result in adult functional and emotional problems and disorders. In this chapter we will focus primarily on sexual abuse during childhood.

Sexual abuse is defined as any type of forced or coerced sexual interaction in which there is a disproportional degree of power and control by the perpetrator or the abuser. The interaction can be assaultive or sexually oriented. In abusive situations the abuser maintains power and control rather than there being equity of control and power. The abuser uses this power to manipulate. There is an element of victim vulnerability with a focus on meeting the needs of the perpetrator rather than considering mutual needs. Safety of the abused is either violated or not considered. This can include physical and or emotional safety and well-being. The victim is the object of the sexual gratification with no reciprocal regard for the total person.

Sexual abuse can be within the family, defined as incestual, or outside of the family. It can be same sex, mixed sex or opposite sex. There is a distinction in childhood abuse of abuse and "play." Generally, to be considered abuse, there must be coercion and more than 5 years of age difference. Although individuals may feel a sense of guilt or shame (sometimes at the suggestion of a counselor or therapist) about childhood experimentation, abuse does not exist from a diagnostic standpoint unless there is an element of coercion without shared power and control.

Recently, there appears to be a disturbing tendency to diagnose the cause of emotional dysphoria as related to childhood sexual abuse without data. This is partly because one of the ways to defend against traumatic childhood experiences is to depersonalize and to repress not only the experience but feelings about the experience. However, in many other types of emotional illness this denial defense mechanism is used. Individuals who are suffering from emotional problems often want to know the reason why and tend to focus on causal factors rather than the here and now and changes in behaviors and attitudes which might develop problem solving and adaptive behaviors which are healthy and therapeutic.

Self help groups have been formed to "heal the child within" and help "victims" of childhood trauma. This can be very helpful and therapeutic. However, group leaders, therapists and individuals themselves must realize that there is the possibility of suggestability. Some counselors state that if there are feelings of doubt, uncertainty, or feelings of uneasiness about one's childhood, there is a probability of sexual abuse. An approach such as this can result in focusing on only one possibility and limit intervention, flexibility and choices.

This is not to discount the fact that childhood sexual abuse is more common than reported in all probability. And, reports have increased in recent years. In one national study in 1985, 27 percent of the females interviewed and 16 percent of the males reported to have been sexually abused as children. Other studies indicate that these figures are too low. It is suggested that eighty percent of all sexual abuse is not reported because of shame, guilt, ignorance, tolerance and or threats if disclosure is made.

Some of the acts included in current literature include breech of privacy in the bathroom or bedroom; subjecting the individual to humiliating sexual comments including one's sexual development; forced cross dressing; intrusive examination of the child's body; fondling or intrusive hugging and kissing; exposing the child to sexually explicit pictures or movies or telling sexual stories; forcing the child to pose nude;

simulation of intercourse or actual intrusive sex with the child including penetration or forcing the child to penetrate another or self with an object; oral stimulation and participation in ritualistic sexual practices.

Sexual abuse of a child results in trauma sometimes because of physical assault or injury but also because of emotional and psychological damage and injury. Many abused individuals experience a loss of trust because they feel they have been taken advantage of by a significant other. Often there are ambivalent feelings of being special as well as feelings of guilt and shame. Fears of abandonment are commonly reported as well as unhealthy forms of dependence in later life.

Sexual abuse frequently takes place during a significant time in the child's development. One of the early and most important stages in childhood development is the development of trust. Erik Erikson stated that it is important not only in relationships to others but in ultimately developing a sense of trust in one's abilities and in developing a sense of self-esteem. Failure to develop trust or the development of mistrust results in feelings of hopelessness, negativity, a sense of separation and alienation and fear. Many of these feelings and traits are reported by those who have been sexually abused as children.

Sexual abuse may be a single event or a continuing process. Often there is a progressive violation of boundaries and barriers. Initially these may be offers of reward or special treatment linked to the abuse or bargaining to break down resistance. The perpetrator commonly rationalizes and attempts to convince the victim that the abuse is normal. The child is often blamed or implicated by the abuser.

Symptoms of abuse vary during various ages and developmental times. These symptoms should be used as guidelines when sexual abuse is suspected, not for diagnostic purposes. A professional should be contacted if you, as a parent or significant other, suspect that a child is being abused. One of the major reasons for this is that disclosure is often traumatic and care must be taken to prevent increased trauma. Bringing past abusive experiences to consciousness from repression can result in decompensation.

Symptoms of ongoing or current sexual abuse can be physical, sexual, intellectual, emotional and behavioral. Small children often display bedwetting, overactive gag responses, nightmares, regression (i.e., acting in an inappropriate immature way), excessive masturbation and sexual preoccupation and language, touching self, forgetfulness, expressions of "feeling dirty," loss of trust, aggression, hyperactivity and or acting out.

If these behaviors and signs develop suddenly or are chronic diagnostic help is recommended.

In later childhood and adolescence there may be such signs as layering of clothing and hand hiding in shirt or blouse sleeves, somatic problems such as severe headaches, sexual promiscuity or seductiveness, expressed feelings of being different or empty, negative self-image and blame, self-hatred with or without self-mutilation, depression, shame, anger, fear of being with a significant other alone, running away, substance abuse, cynicism and a vulnerability for cult involvement.

In adulthood there are various signs which suggest the possibility of childhood sexual abuse. These include intolerance of being touched by another, psychosomatic illnesses, sleep and appetite disturbances, sexual promiscuity or inhibited sexual desire, amnesia and problems with recalling one's childhood (As was discussed, one symptom alone is not sufficient to diagnose CSA.), feelings of emotional dissociation, blunted emotions, lack of emotional feelings, distrust of others, sexualization of everyday situations and events, a tendency to be attracted to older powerful or abusive partners, addictions, self-mutilation, passive aggressive behaviors and attitudes, depression and feelings of isolation.

Many of these symptoms are common among individuals who are suffering from other emotional problems or illness however a disproportionately large number of these particular symptoms suggest sexual abuse as a child.

Related disorders include mood disorder, anxiety and panic disorders, substance abuse and according to some researchers, personality disorders, especially borderline personality disorder (see chapter XXVIII on personality disorders). In treatment these other disorders should also be addressed. In some cases the sexual abuse issue should not be explored until later. An example of this is someone who is depressed and has been hospitalized following a suicide attempt. Sexual abuse as a child may be known or suspected but the priority is to alleviate depression, stabilize the individual and eliminate the risk of suicide.

Adolescents who are severely depressed are often hospitalized or treated with intensive outpatient therapy. In many cases there is evidence of sexual abuse. Of course, immediate steps must be taken if the abuse is suspected to be current and ongoing. However, therapists often make the mistake of focusing on the abuse immediately rather than alleviating depression and stabilizing the individual. The development of ego defenses is often necessary before bringing into consciousness the traumatic events and experiences. Denial, repression and blockage are all ego defenses and should not be disturbed until the abused individual is emotionally able to deal with the trauma.

Various treatment models are used in dealing with childhood sexual abuse. Some therapists focus on the result of the trauma and abuse. This model might be called the "victim" approach. Focus is on the damage done, the feelings experienced due to the abuse and the resulting personality relationship and functional impairments. There is a tendency to emphasize not only the traumatic impact of the abuse but also the chronicity of the impairment. Healing the "victim" is emphasized. This is an interesting approach because it tends to make the person who was abused powerless and vulnerable. This appears to be the same situation in which the abused was during the abuse. When the "healer" takes control of the "healing process," the similarities between the here and now therapeutic situation and relationship and the sexual abuse during childhood become more similar.

A second approach focuses on the individual's strength and capacity to self-heal. This model might be called the "survivor model." The focus is on the present rather than the past and on moving on with one's life rather than focusing on past injuries and violations. Labels are usually not utilized. Dysfunctional behaviors are identified and changes made which result in more adaptive functioning. There is the concept of transcending suffering which makes the abused person the ultimate victor. This model focuses on behavior (rather than "victim traits") and ways to overcome problems.

In the following chapters we discuss various treatment modes and the subject of choosing a therapist if therapy is warranted. In the treatment of childhood sexual abuse a few suggestions should be made. The first is that the therapist must not create more trauma than help by recreating a therapeutic situation that resembles the abusive dynamics. This is not to say that in therapy there will never be a sense of dysphoria or stress. In fact, the skillful therapist has an obligation to help the individual identify feelings and problems and deal with the stress. However, many people who begin to make progress by examining repressed feelings leave therapy before there is any real improvement because these feelings are so painful. Treatment of sexual abuse (a form of Post Traumatic Stress Disorder) is based on overcoming denial, repression and minimizing; recalling past experiences; confronting the pain and rage; forgiveness and healing; and integration and going forward. A patriarch/

matriarch model should be avoided. The individual must be provided with an assurance of safety and control. The client must be encouraged to discuss experienced levels of anxiety, intrusiveness and discomfort and the therapeutic process. Involvement in group therapy might be beneficial with the caution to consider whether the model is victim or survivor focused.

The impact of childhood sexual abuse in the family depends on the relationships, the type and chronicity of the abuse and the family system itself. Impact on the abused is most severe when the abuse takes place over a period of time, the abuser is a parent, the disclosure is not acknowledged and immediate help is not provided.

Families often dissolve once the abuse is discovered or disclosed. Relationships usually change with one or another member becoming alienated. Blame may be directed at the abuser or the abused. In all situations there is impact, adjustment and trauma. Often this occurs suddenly based on disclosure, although suspicions prior to discovery and disclosure are common. Crisis often creates anger, fear, anxiety and emotional reactions which are not very functional. Family members must be aware that denial is often used to avoid pain and postpone or eliminate the need for change.

As a family member, focus on your own feelings and needs. Although you may not be the abused or the abuser, you may experience feelings of loss of trust, shame, confusion, hurt and depression. Do not repress these feelings. Acknowledge that these feelings and emotions are real and if necessary seek professional help and encourage others in the family who need help to participate in therapy. Certainly, as a non-abusing parent or significant other of a child who is being sexually abused (or physically abused) you have a responsibility to protect the child.

Chapter XIX

SEXUAL DYSFUNCTIONS

S exual disorders are divided into two categories. The first, which was discussed in Chapter XVII, is the Paraphilia Disorder in which there is intense arousal in response to situations or objects which do not normally cause arousal. This arousal interferes, in one way or another, with affectionate sexual activity with another person. On the other hand, the sexual dysfunctions cause inhibition in sexual desire or completion of the sexual response cycle. This is not considered a mental disorder if the cause of the inhibition or the completion of the sexual cycle is physical or medical in nature. There are a number of physical and organic disorders which result in sexual dysfunction. Sexual dysfunction can also be a side effect of medication or toxicity. Because of this, consultation with a physician is recommended to rule out these causes.

The normal sexual cycle has four phases. (Some people add a fifth stage, i.e., putting on one's socks.) During the first stage or phase a desire for sexual activity develops based on fantasies. The second stage is that of excitement. Two things take place during this phase. The individual experiences a sense of sexual pleasure or anticipation as well as physiological changes. In the male, an erection begins. In the female there is vasocongestion of the pelvis, vaginal lubrication and swelling. The third stage is that of orgasm which is the peaking of sexual pleasure with release of tension. The final stage is that of resolution with more complete muscular relaxation and a sense of well-being. Following orgasm, males experience a refractory response during which time an additional erection and orgasm is impossible. This period of time varies with the individual. Females are able to have multiple complete orgasms without this period of refraction, almost immediately.

Sexual dysfunction may occur in one or more of these stages resulting in incompletion of the cycle. Usually both the physiological response and a sense of pleasure are inhibited. In order to be classified as a sexual dysfunction due to emotional or mental illness there must be a psychological factor involved; however, there may also be a biogenic cause. The

109

dysfunction can be long-lasting or acquired after a period of adequate or normal sexual functioning. It may be in certain situations or with certain partners or generalized. It may occur during masturbation.

In some situations such as hyposexual desire, performance may be sporadic or occasional. There is often accompanying feelings of anxiety or shame in situations of nonperformance. Fear of failure and avoidance are common. The individual frequently self-monitors and becomes acutely aware of his or her partner's responses adding to the tension and anxiety and thus contributing to the dysfunction. This is similar to the anticipatory anxiety found in panic disorders. Problems in communication with the partner, feelings of anger and failure, and withdrawal add to the dysphoria. Often the partner develops feelings of blame.

Sexual dysfunction disorders can develop at any age, however the most common age for the symptoms to appear is during the 20's and 30's following the establishment of sexual relations. Problems with erection are usually later in life. Premature ejaculation is more common during the early years of sexual activity.

The course varies. Sexual dysfunction may be chronic or episodic. The greatest area of impairment is in relationships although individuals who are experiencing sexual dysfunction may experience forms of depression which are pervasive and effect other areas of their lives.

Sexual dysfunction does not appear to be genetic. It is, more likely, related to characterological and situational factors. Individuals who have placed upon themselves high expectations of sexual performance or suffer from fears of inadequacy or rejection are more predisposed to develop sexual dysfunction as are individuals who have developed negative attitudes about sex or have had negative experiences.

Sexual dysfunctions are probably very common, especially in mild forms. Twenty percent of the population is speculated to suffer from low sexual appetite or asexuality. Thirty percent of the male population reportedly suffer from premature ejaculation and 30% of the female population have inhibited orgasm.

Lack of sexual desire can be the result of prolonged stress, anxiety or depression. It can also be the result of long term abstinence or repressed feelings of anger and hostility. Women and men often express different reasons for lack of interest in sex. Women appear to be more influenced by emotional perceptions than men. Both sexes report lack of interest as a concurrent symptom with relationship or marital problems. Both sexes may suffer from inhibited sexual desire due to disorders such as diabetes or illnesses which involve pain. If sexual dysfunction continues over time, or is independent from situational factors, physical causes can be suspected.

Personality disorders may also coexist or can be a major causal factor in dysfunction. The way we view relationships and interact with others is dependent, in part, on our personality style, our own goals and needs, and our past experiences. Individuals who have been abused in the past frequently have problems with trust and intimacy. Antisocial individuals and those suffering from narcissistic disorders may have problems with developing empathy and reciprocity in sexual relationships. Those with low self-esteem may see themselves as undesirable and thus develop avoidant and negative attitudes and self images. Research has documented the fact that human sexual response is psychological in nature with emotions, perceptions, ideas, and belief systems controlling physiological responses.

Sexual desire disorders require that there exists persistent or recurrent deficit or absence of sexual fantasies sufficient to develop a desire for sexual activity. There is also sexual aversion disorder where the individual avoids or has an aversion to genital sexual contact with a partner.

Sexual excitement disorders include female arousal problems and male erectile disorder. In both disorders there is a failure to attain or maintain the physiological state of excitement until completion of activity. In the male the erection is not maintained. In the woman the lubrication-swelling is not maintained. Women who have this problem usually also have problems with orgasm. This problem effects up to 33% of the female population. Male erectile dysfunction or impotence can be primary where the individual has never been able to maintain an erection long enough for vaginal insertion or secondary where the condition has developed after a period of successful maintained excitement. Primary impotence is rare. Secondary impotence is more common with some researchers reporting an increase in anxiety and concern about the disorder over age 40 when males tend to fear loss of virility. (Impotence, however, does not regularly occur with aging males as a matter of course.)

There is a difference of opinion as to the organic as opposed to the psychological factors involved in impotence. Of course, both conditions can exist. Diseases which can be causal include cardiovascular, renal, and urological, hepatic, pulmonary, nutritional, endocrine, neurological disorders; a response to medication and toxicity; and surgical procedure responses. Individuals who abuse alcohol and other mood altering drugs frequently suffer from lack of desire and arousal. Psychotropic, anti-hypertensive and antiandrogen drugs can also cause impotence or problems with sexual functioning. Most outpatient treatment centers for sexual dysfunction require an extensive physical evaluation. The intensity and invasiveness of these assessments vary a great deal. A complete history is important in determining the cause of impotence. If a male reports erections at times when not planning on intercourse, morning erections, sporadic impotence, adequate erections when masturbating or with partners other than the usual one, organic causes are unlikely and extensive diagnostic procedures should probably be avoided. In cases where organic causes are identified there are commonly psychological components which should be treated or at least discussed, such as fear of failure and anticipatory anxiety.

In females psychological factors, of course, can also be coexisting. Both males and females should explore their feelings regarding sex including childhood messages and family of origin beliefs and percepts. Sexual images are related to past experiences and situations often in early childhood years. Gender identification, according to many, is learned behavior as is sexual stimulation. Maintained excitement or arousal is dependent on these images and fantasies. Emotions such as fear, anxiety and anger or moral prohibition can result in limited desire and or arousal and inhibited performance.

Female orgasm disorders include primary non-orgasmic dysfunction where an orgasm has never been experienced and secondary where an orgasm has been experienced however there is currently a persistent and recurrent delay or absence of orgasm following a normal excitement phase. Primary dysfunction is considered rare in women over age 35. The incidence of orgasm increases with age. There is a greater percentage of unmarried women than married women who have never experienced an orgasm. More women complain of difficulty in reaching orgasm than in not having an orgasm. Problems with excitement and orgasm both occur in some cases.

Psychosexual issues, related to female excitement and or orgasm dysfunction can include fear of impregnation and pregnancy, hostility, guilt, fear of lack of control and dominance, and cultural and social beliefs and mores.

Male orgasm dysfunction is often identified as retarded ejaculation.

Ejaculation may be delayed or absent. Inhibited orgasm among males is much less common than premature ejaculation and impotence. Males with obsessive compulsive personality disorders, however, tend to be predisposed for inhibited male orgasm. This disorder can also occur following genitourinary surgery and can be a side effect of Parkinson's disease and some types of medication including antihypertensive drugs. Inhibited male orgasm appears to be related, in many cases, to rather severe psychological issues and problems. Individuals who suffer from this disorder tend to be rigid with views that sex is unhealthy. Other causes can be loss of interest in partner, fear of pregnancy, or repressed hostility toward females.

Premature ejaculation is defined as the persistent or recurrent ejaculation with minimum sexual stimulation before ejaculation is desired. It can occur before, upon or shortly after, penetration. Factors such as age of the male, novelty of the act and frequency should be considered in deciding if an individual suffers from this disorder. This disorder is more common with college age men than those with less education, according to some research. Social situations and conditions where in the past rapidity of orgasm was necessary or desired has been identified as a factor as has anxiety in general. A stressful marriage can contribute to this situation.

A fourth category of sexual dysfunction is that of painful sexual disorder in which either the male or female experiences pain prior to, during, or after intercourse. This is known as dyspareunia. Vaginismus is the recurrent or involuntary spasm of the vagina that inhibits coitus. For the female these two problems are sometimes coexistent. These diagnoses are not appropriate when organic or physical causes alone are found. In some cases there are organic abnormalities. Pain may be associated with postmenopause and thinning of the vaginal mucosa and lubrication or gland infection. However, pain may also result from anxiety and tension causing an involuntary tightening of the vaginal muscles. Dyspareunia is uncommon in males. If it does occur it is usually organic. Peyronie's disease can be a causal disorder in males. Past sexual trauma or psychosexual conflict beliefs in women can cause vaginismus.

Other sexual disorders include marked and distressful feelings of inadequacy about sexual performance or size and shape of genital organs, distress over nonparaphilic sexual addiction, and marked distress about one's sexual orientation.

A number of new approaches have been developed to treat sexual dysfunctions. The first step is to determine the nature of the disorder and whether the cause is physical, psychological or both. In some cases, where the dysfunction is primarily organic, secondary persistent problems of a psychological nature exist and continue to exist after treatment.

Sexual dysfunction often causes marital conflict and interpersonal relationship problems. There may be resentments, feelings of guilt, anger, shame and withdrawal. Identifying the problems and discussing feelings is primary not only in treating the dysfunction but in reestablishing intimacy. Sexual dysfunction is usually a joint or dual dysfunction in that there is not an element of mutual sexual satisfaction. Hypoactive sexual desire, for example, results in lack of desire or deficient desire. Sexual partners, of course, often vary as far as appetite and desire, however inability or difficulty in maintaining an erection or having an orgasm certainly can result in lack of mutual satisfaction and intimacy.

Because there is often hesitancy to discuss sexual feelings, needs and satisfaction or denial, sexual dysfunction problems are frequently not identified. This is unfortunate. While outcome varies, treatment has proven to be very effective in many cases. Outcome is guarded where there is severe marital conflict and where sexual dysfunction is chronic. In situations where there are problems with dependency, codependency, hostility, unhealthy sexual attitudes and beliefs, problems with impulse, unresolved sexual orientation conflicts, mood disorders and characterological disorder problems, treatment is more difficult. Often sexual dysfunction is a symptom of other problems. Treatment approaches include dual-sex therapy where the couple participates; hypnotherapy to decrease anxiety; behavior therapy based on changing learned behaviors; group therapy to explore interpersonal relationship style problems and needs; analytical therapy using psychodynamic Freudian techniques; and individual therapy.

Chapter XX

DELUSIONAL PARANOID DISORDER

D*SM IV* describes delusional disorder as a disorder where there exists a persistent non-bizarre delusion. Other than the delusions and related aspects behavior is not odd or bizarre. Paranoid thoughts or ideations can be present in schizophrenia and as the pervasive symptom of paranoid personality disorder. Paranoid delusions can also result from amphetamine, cannabis and cocaine intoxication. In fact, reports of paranoia are quite common among those who are chronic users of mood altering drugs, especially cocaine. However, in the case of delusional disorder the delusions are not due to other mental disorders such as schizophrenia, drug toxicity or personality disorder.

Delusional themes in this disorder vary. Erotomanic type themes are those in which the individual believes that they are loved by another, usually one of higher status such as a rock star or famous political figure. The love is one of idealized romance and usually spiritual union rather than sexual in nature. Attempts to contact the person, even though the idealized love object is a stranger, often take place. Stalking and surveillance are common. Sometimes there are efforts to rescue the individual from imagined dangers. In many cases the behaviors of the person with the erotomanic beliefs become a harassment.

A second type of paranoid delusion is that of grandiosity. The individual often believes that they have special powers. In other cases the sufferer may believe they are related to a famous or wealthy person.

A third type is that of jealousy with the related, unfounded belief that a spouse or significant other is untrue. Strained relations develop when the delusional partner attempts to restrict the autonomy of the other person. Physical assaults of the suspected partner or imagined "lover" may result.

The most common type of paranoid delusion is that of persecution. Themes include being cheated, spied on, poisoned or drugged, harassed and/or slandered. The individual suffering from these delusions tends to be angry and resentful and on occasion violent.

Somatic delusions are another form of paranoid disorder with the individual believing that they emit a foul odor, have internal parasites, are ugly or misshapen or have organs which are not functioning.

In order to be classified as Delusional Paranoid Disorder the delusions must have existed for at least one month. Age of onset is usually in middle or late adulthood. The course of the disorder varies. In some cases there is complete remission. However, persecutory delusions tend to be chronic.

Usually the individual who is suffering from these delusions is able to function occupationally. The areas of impairment tend to be marital and social. When the behaviors and attitudes of the individual suffering from the disorder become obsessive and/or compulsive, marital and family dysfunction follow.

Predisposing factors include immigration, migration, physical disabilities including deafness or severe social stresses. These factors tend to be such that the individual does not understand or relate to the social situation and environment. Paranoid delusions may be a form of defending against imagined injury, ridicule or harm. However, in the case of this disorder the beliefs are delusional and not founded on reality.

Delusional disorder is uncommon with more females than males developing the symptoms. Individuals who have avoidant, schizoid or paranoid personality disorders are more likely to develop delusional paranoid disorder than the general population. Personality Disorders will be discussed in another chapter. Delusional disorder symptoms may also be present in the early stages of dementia. In schizophrenia, paranoid type, hallucinations are prominent or delusions bizarre in contrast to delusional disorders where there are usually not hallucinations or bizarre delusions. Nonbizarre delusions may occur as secondary symptoms in a mood disorder.

Paranoid personality disorder differs from delusional paranoid disorder in that there are no delusions. The individual suffering from this personality disorder tends to be suspicious and mistrusting of others. Because these individuals tend to deny that the suspicions and mistrust are unrealistic, they are resistant to change. They often hold resentments, are judgemental and angry and tend to be litigious and easily offended. They can be hypervigilant, guarded, refuse to accept blame or responsibility, secretive, jealous and have problems enjoying life or relaxing. Hostile, suspicious traits result in the individual becoming isolative and rejected.

Individuals suffering from paranoid delusions or personality disorder tend to have problems with dependency and intimacy. They often distain the weak, soft or defective. In many cases the objects of their disdain resemble their own weaknesses or imagined self. It has been noted by historians that Hitler's inner circle physically resembled those they persecuted rather than the blond, blue eyed Aryans they admired. Individuals who are paranoid commonly are preoccupied with detail and find fault in the insignificant. They tend to personalize things which would be ignored by those not suffering from the disorder.

Living with a family member who is pathologically paranoid is difficult. Medication usually is not effective in that the delusions or beliefs are not psychotic in nature. Psychotropic medication is not effective with individuals who are suffering from a personality disorder. Individuals with the disorder usually do not admit that they are having problems and resist treatment and change. Thus, it is up to the family member to act. The key phrase is "act" rather than "react." The following recommendations are made:

1) Determine how the family member's paranoia impacts on you. Analyze how the individual's attitudes and behaviors effect you socially, financially, emotionally and physically. Is it causing you to become withdrawn and isolative yourself? Does it effect your relationship with family and friends? Do you have to apologize for the family member? Are you embarrassed? Are your personal needs met including the need for understanding, intimacy and love? Are you becoming physically or emotionally ill because of the paranoia of a spouse or significant other? Have you been or are you being physically or emotionally abused? Answer these questions honestly.

2) Define your level of tolerance.

3) Decide what action to take. This may require professional help. It is best to realize that the prognosis for change in the family member may be poor. However, an accurate diagnosis as to the nature and severity of the disorder is best made by a professional. The role of the therapist should be to help you determine how you are affected and what your needs are as well as evaluate the situation. The individual who suffers from delusional paranoid disorder or personality disorder has problems with trust and will

often resist involvement in treatment. Behavior therapy will be resisted as too intrusive.

4) If you decide to stay in the relationship a few suggestions may be of benefit. Be straightforward, honest and direct, focusing on your own feelings and how identifiable paranoid behaviors impact on you. Delusional accusations must be discussed realistically without humiliating the family member. Limits can be set and consequences discussed however it must be remembered that attacking the paranoid family member or making them feel weak and helpless will only exacerbate the symptoms.

5) Discussing your feelings in individual therapy and realizing that your needs can be met in many ways is also suggested.

Chapter XXI

OBSESSIVE COMPULSIVE DISORDER

D*SM IV* defines Obsessive Compulsive Disorder as obsessions or compulsions that cause marked distress, are time consuming or interfere significantly with a person's life either occupationally, socially or in relationships with others. Obsessions are thoughts, ideas or images that are experienced as intrusive and senseless. An example is the idea of a parent having the impulse to kill a newborn infant or fears that she or he may in some way intentionally harm the child. As a defense the individual attempts to ignore or suppress the thoughts or impulses. Obsessions are recognized as senseless and the product of one's mind however in OCD they continue and cause distress.

Compulsions are repetitive behaviors performed in response to an obsession in a set, stereotyped manner. The behaviors are attempts to neutralize or prevent discomfort or some dreaded event however the ritual is actually not a realistic preventative action. Again, as in the case of obsessions, the response is recognized as excessive or unreasonable. No pleasure is derived from the obsession or compulsion, although it may temporarily relieve tension. Common compulsions are counting, checking, touching objects, repeating phrases or prayers and handwashing.

Some theorists believe that obsessions and compulsions are related to repressed guilt and that individuals who are judgemental and have a rigid outlook on life tend to be prone to developing obsessive or compulsive behaviors. Symptoms of depression and anxiety are often prevalent among people suffering from OCD as is phobic avoidance.

The disorder usually begins around adolescence or early adulthood. Chronic stress may exacerbate symptoms. Impairment depends on the particular obsession or compulsion and the severity as well as other psychological disorders which may also exist. In some cases, the obsessions and compulsions become so intrusive and pervasive that everyday routine functions are difficult or impossible to carry out. Use of alcohol to self-medicate and control or attempt to control mood and anxiety is not uncommon. The disorder, which is equally common in men and women, appears to be fairly extensive in the general population in a mild form.

Many theories as to the cause of OCD have been presented over the years. Freud initially presented the idea that phobic and obsessive compulsive disorders were closely related with thoughts and emotions, as counter measures in response to repressed urges and desires unacceptable to the superego. Learning theory focuses on obsessions and compulsions as methods of avoidance and displacement. The obsession is a conditioned stimulus to anxiety. The compulsion, according to this theory, reduces the anxiety related to obsessional thoughts. In other words, it is an attempt to defocus or diminish the intrusive power of the obsession. Other theorists focus on the possibility of organicity and pathological processes in the central nervous system.

Other theorists identify characterological traits where control is necessary or primary. There appears to be some evidence to support the observation that these individuals do attempt to control their emotions and environment more so than the general public and that they are cautious, deliberate and sometimes overly analytical. Logic rather than emotion is stressed. They tend to be reliable and conscientious although they may lack flexibility, creativity and imagination. They like structure and predictable situations and relationships. Security is important to them.

Many of these traits are desirable and do not, in and of themselves, reflect abnormality, unless the traits become extreme and interfere with functional and adaptive ability. Obsessive compulsive personality disorder is defined as a pattern of inflexibility and perfectionism which tends to be dysfunctional. Symptoms include preoccupation with detail, with loss of insight as to the basic objective; unreasonable demands for compliance by others; excessive devotion to work; indecisiveness; being overly conscientious; restricted ability to express affection; lack of generosity; and saving worthless or worn out objects.

Three forms of treatment are commonly used to treat obsessive compulsive disorders—psychotherapy, behavior therapy and medication.

Individuals suffering from OCD are more likely to experience feelings of shame, guilt and dysphoria than those suffering from paranoid disorders. Often they are able to conceal their obsessions and compulsions. They may attempt to rationalize to others although they themselves recognize the counterproductive and senselessness of the thoughts and behaviors. Unlike those suffering from paranoia, others are usually not viewed with distrust or disdain. Thus, interpersonal relationships can develop and be rewarding and satisfying. However, significant others may experience concern and empathy. Being supportive and understanding is of course helpful. Confronting the individual and urging them to "stop it" is not usually a productive strategy. Urging that they seek professional help is a better idea.

Chapter XXII

ADJUSTMENT DISORDERS

There are two primary components to adjustment disorders. The first is that there was an identifiable stressor that occurred within three months of the onset of the disorder. The second is that the response to the stress or stressors is maladaptive. The maladaptive response has to have impaired occupational abilities (including school), social activities or relationships or the response must be in excess of the normal or expected reactions. In order to be diagnosed as an adjustment disorder the response must be distinct from a tendency to overreact maladaptively or as the result of another mental disorder.

Examples of stressors include divorce, business losses, termination of employment, chronic illness or marital problems. They can also be life stage events such as leaving home, getting married, or entering retirement. Losses such as the death of a child or parent can also be a stressor.

The distinction between adjustment disorder as a mental illness, and adjustment to a stressor which is not considered pathological is in the way the individual responds to the stressor. There is a difference between normal grief following a death or a loss and adjustment disorder with depression. In order for the adjustment to be considered as "mental illness" the response must be maladaptive and present a predominant clinical picture.

Adjustment disorders may occur at any age. The onset may be immediate such as is often the case following job termination or may develop over a period of time up to three months following the stressor. If the symptoms persist for longer than six months the diagnosis is chronic. If the disturbance lasts for less than six months, it is considered acute. The prevalence of the disorder is common.

Adjustment disorders have symptoms in common with phase of life problem diagnoses but with the unexpected, abnormal or impairing response. There are also similarities to post traumatic stress disorder (PTSD) however in the case of PTSD the event experienced is outside of the range of normal human experience.

Types of adjustment disorder include adjustment disorder with anxiety, depressed mood, disturbance of conduct, mixed disturbance of emotions and conduct, and mixed anxiety and depressed mood.

The degree of maladaption varies with the individual and the particular stressor or stressors. Some individual's maladaptive response is more severe than others. The severity of the impairment is related to many factors including past experiences, support systems, ego strengths and abilities, and personal resources. Acute trauma stressors such as being fired from a job are different from chronic stressors such as ongoing marital conflict. The timing of a stressor may also be significant. For example, the death of a parent prior to one's marriage would appear to create a significant response. The individual's particular situation and the combination of psychosocial stressors must be taken into account when attempting to understand the disorder and predict outcome.

Treatment is available for adjustment disorders and must be considered based on the probability that the resolution of the symptoms will probably take place more rapidly with professional help. There are times, in the opinion of this author, when everyone would benefit from therapy. Therapy does not have to be long term or intrusive. Focusing on the current situation and developing more adaptive responses is recommended. Relief and alleviation of the symptoms is primary. Too often therapists focus on other issues and factors. Of course, the individual might benefit from more extensive therapy such as growth therapy, however, this should not be the priority. Once the primary symptoms are alleviated, other issues can be and possibly should be discussed.

Recommendations for family members include:

1) Being available and supportive.
2) Examining how the stressor impacted on you as a family member and identifying your own feelings. You might benefit from becoming involved in therapy.
3) Encouraging the individual to seek help for themselves. Too often individuals "tough it out" and suffer for too long a period without hope, direction, and insight on how to make adaptive changes. One of the first and most important steps in personal growth and happiness is to realize that we have choices, and can change the way we react and adjust to the world around us and to our situation. Professional help is sometimes needed to identify and explore better ways of reacting and responding.

Chapter XXIII

SCHIZOPHRENIA

S chizophrenia is one of the most debilitating of the mental illnesses. This is because of the dysfunctional and often bizarre, inappropriate and disorganized behaviors during episodes; the chronicity of the disorder; and the fact that often there is a resistance to treatment and medical compliance.

Another factor is that onset is usually during adolescence or early adulthood. This is significant in that individuals during these life stages have usually not developed a sense of identity, do not have career skills and may not have the support systems available to them that older individuals have. Developmentally, adolescence and early adulthood is a time of gaining a sense of self and separating from family. It is a time of emancipation. Chronic mental illness tends to interfere with this process, and as will be discussed, creates real problems in the family system and with individual family members.

Individuals in adolescence and early adulthood tend to be very sensitive to the opinions of others and have a need to be accepted. Any hint of inadequacy or imperfection is rejected. Mental and physical problems and illnesses are especially dreaded in that they are threatening to ego and sense of self. Because of this, individuals in these life stages tend to deny. This, of course, results in resistance to treatment.

Treatment problems also arise because of failure to diagnose. A number of other mental disorders have similar symptoms. Psychotic episodes, features, and symptoms may be secondary to organicity, mood disorder or drug use. Of course, it is possible for an individual with schizophrenia to be suffering from other mental disorders; however an adequate diagnosis is necessary for treatment. It is difficult in diagnosis to differentiate between preschizophrenic symptoms and other forms of psychosis. Diagnosing schizophrenia in an adolescent/young adult population is also complicated because identity and personality characteristics are not as well established as is the case in older individuals. Histrionic or paranoid personality disorder traits can present as preschizophrenic. Schizotypal personality disorder also can be confused with schizophrenia as can schizoaffective disorder. These disorders and the differences between them and schizophrenia will be discussed later in this chapter.

A diagnosis of schizophrenia requires the presence of psychotic symptoms during the active stage of at least one month. There must be at least two of the following symptoms: delusions; hallucinations; catatonic behavior; disorganized speech; or negative symptoms. Thus, delusions and hallucinations do not have to both be present. (Delusions are thoughts that are irrational. Hallucinations are sensory disturbances like hearing voices which do not exist or seeing people or objects which are non-existent.) If either the delusion or hallucination is bizarre or prominent, schizophrenia can be suspected. However, other mental illnesses must be ruled out as discussed previously. A third requirement for the diagnosis of schizophrenia is that during the episode there must be impairment in functional areas such as work, social relations and self-care.

There are various stages of schizophrenia. The active stage when symptoms are most obvious and severe must have lasted at least one month with the disturbance (including prodromal or residual symptoms) having lasted at least six months. In other words, this is not a short term disturbance of thought processes such as found in delirium. Residual symptoms can include isolation and withdrawal, peculiar behavior, impaired hygiene, impaired functional ability, thought digressions, odd beliefs, delusions and anhedonia.

Types of schizophrenia include catatonic type; disorganized type; paranoid type; undifferentiated type; and residual type. Symptoms of the catatonic type include catatonic stupor (mutism or lack of reaction to the environment), catatonic negativism (motionless resistance to commands), catatonic rigidity (rigid posture), catatonic excitement or catatonic posturing (bizarre or inappropriate posturing).

As would be expected, the symptoms of disorganized schizophrenia include disorganized thought processes and flat or inappropriate affect. Paranoid schizophrenics are preoccupied with systematized paranoid delusions or have paranoid hallucinations with a single theme. There are no signs of incoherence, loose associations, catatonia or grossly disturbed behavior. Undifferentiated type symptoms are less extreme than those observed in catatonic type, disorganized type and paranoid type.

Schizophrenia differs from delirium in that, while there may be disorganized thinking in delirium and rambling and incoherent speech, these symptoms are often acute and tend to fluctuate over the course of a day. In delirium, an organic factor (such as specific infections or metabolic disease) is suspected or the delirium is postoperative or related to drug intoxication or withdrawal.

Individuals suffering from dementia tend to have problems with memory (usually not present in schizophrenia although testing of memory functions is often either difficult or impossible during the active stage of schizophrenia) and abstract thinking impairment. Again, in dementia organic causes are either known or suspected. In schizophrenia there is also more likelihood of disorganization and bizarre and inappropriate behaviors or hallucinations.

In schizoaffective disorder there exists a mood disturbance; however schizophrenic individuals are also often depressed confusing diagnosis. In cases of depression or bipolar disorder psychotic symptoms may be present; however they are secondary to the mood disorder. Frequently the psychotic features appear during the later or more severe stages of the mood disorder. Psychotic features may be observed in various personality disorders; however, they are not as extreme as in schizophrenia and do not impair functioning as severely as in the case of schizophrenia. Also they tend to be transient whereas with schizophrenia, during the active stage, the disturbance lasts for at least a week. In the case of personality disorders, behaviors and attitudes tend to be neurotic rather than bizarre and disorganized. There are no symptoms of loose association and the individual does not become incoherent.

Again, because psychotic symptoms are common in other forms of mental illness, an accurate diagnosis is required. This is also necessary to provide treatment and to help the family in developing coping mechanisms.

Schizophrenia is equally common among the sexes. While genetic factors have been suggested in the development of schizophrenia, it must be stressed that non-genetic factors also exist. Associated features of schizophrenia include ritualistic behaviors, agitation, concrete thinking, disturbed mood, somatic concerns, depersonalization, and eccentricity in dress and appearance. Mood swings are common with possibility of the individual becoming aggressive, assaultive and violent during the active stage. These behaviors and the fact that they are often not related to particular stressors or environmental factors tends to create extreme anxiety in the family. Schizophrenic acting out might be compared to the behaviors common during active manic stages in bipolar disorder.

The active phase of schizophrenia is commonly often preceded by a prodromal stage during which there is a deterioration in functions and a display of active phase symptoms. This is a warning to the family and significant others. Family members who have lived with individuals who are schizophrenic become quite accurate in their observations and awareness of symptoms. This is good, in a way, because treatment can be recommended. However, some theorists suggest that vigilance and anxiety in the family system may tend to precipitate episodes. Stress and hostility and critical comments on the part of significant others as well as over involvement have been identified as factors which may lead to relapse. Of course, as is well understood, living with a person who may become psychotic results in a tremendous amount of concern, tension, fear, confusion and often anger. These feelings and responses are common among family members and significant others who live with or are in a close relationship to those who have rage and manic episodes, become psychotic due to other mental disorders or become abusive and irrational because of drug use and intoxication.

The most common course of schizophrenia is one of acute exacerbation (recurrence of active phase symptoms) with residual (or less severe) symptoms between episodes. This is not to say that individuals suffering from schizophrenia cannot lead useful, full and functional lives. However, compliance with treatment is necessary. Individuals who are schizophrenic often resist taking antipsychotic medication. This is similar to the common occurrence of individuals who are bipolar and also medically incompliant. A frequent complaint is that the side effects of the medications are distasteful and intolerable.

Antipsychotic medication (neuroleptics) are used to order thought processes, decrease motor activity, reduce hallucinations and delusions, and reduce anxiety and tension. The most serious side effect is the possible development of extrapyramidal symptoms or Parkinsonian Syndrome which includes muscular rigidity of limbs and face, slowness or scarcity of movements and in some cases jerking and spasms. About 5 percent of patients who take neuroleptics develop tardive dyskinesia. Symptoms include a sucking like puckering of the lips, tongue chewing, twisting and stereotypal extremity movements. Of course, this is terrifying to the individual about to begin taking antipsychotic medication. Especially, because medication is usually recommended for an extended period. The good news is that extrapyramidal symptoms (and other less extreme side effects such as dry mouth, blurred vision, insomnia and nausea) tend to disappear after a period of time. Also, tardive dyskinesia can be guarded against by concurrent use of antiparkinsonian medication. However, it is important to stress the need for continued supervision by a medical doctor who is aware of the dangers and is available and able to monitor response to medication.

Treatment is normally based on a combination of medication and psychotherapy. Clinicians are now beginning to emphasize the need for "psychological rehabilitation." This is because the recidivism rate is so high and because of the chronicity of the disorder. While it may be possible to control and possible to even limit the severity of the symptoms during the active stage of the disorder, too often individuals who are suffering from schizophrenia lead second class lives. In the case of individuals who are afflicted with the disorder at an early age, they have not developed adequate ego defenses and support systems, often lack social and job skills, internalize feelings of self-hatred and low self-worth, have no concept of self and lack a sense of identity and lead a life of anticipatory anxiety, depression and dysphoria.

Family members tend to experience guilt, fear, anxiety and anger. Individuals with schizophrenia tend to appear and disappear. Often they spend time in psychiatric or residential facilities only to return home and regress. Family members tend to have ambivalent feelings. They feel responsible but unconsciously wish for release of responsibility.

Recommendations for family members include:

1) Recognizing the importance of professional help and an accurate, valid diagnosis.
2) Education. It is important to understand the signs, symptoms, cause and treatment of schizophrenia. It is beyond the scope of this book to discuss these issues in depth however there are many sources available. There are support groups for family members of schizophrenics; however a professional in the field of mental health can provide you with data on management techniques and how to best deal with your own emotions as well as appropriate and therapeutic responses to the individual who is schizophrenic.

Specific suggestions on management, relationship and coping mechanisms include:

1) Recognize that you did not cause the disorder and cannot cure it. Recent research discounts the notion that schizophrenia is "caused" by a dominant mother and a passive, unavailable father.

2) Recognize the possibility for recurrence of symptoms.

3) Realize that it is not uncommon for the individual who is suffering from schizophrenia to be in denial. It is also common for family members to be in denial. While it is important to stress the need for professional help, it is probably not possible to overcome denial on the part of the family member by yourself. You can improve reality testing by discussing with the individual behaviors and how these behaviors (during periods of the active stage of the disorder) impact on you and the family. An intervention with other family members directed by a professional might help.

4) Be supportive but not enabling. Set limits on your involvement physically, financially and emotionally.

5) Recognize the need for rehabilitation. Often residential or intensive outpatient care is required to develop social, career and daily living skills. Some of these are private and are funded by insurance payments. However, there are public facilities. Hopefully, society will realize the cost, both financial and emotional, of mental illness and provide better and more effective treatment. Intensive outpatient care has been emphasized recently with encouraging cost benefit statistics.

6) While particular procedures, including lowering of stimulation and arousal during an active stage of the disorder and supportive interaction and family involvement, may help, it is often not beneficial or desirable to have the individual live at home. An assessment of your situation and needs, the prognosis for relapse, and the individual's needs, resources and behaviors should be made, with the help of a professional, to develop a long range plan. Too often family members live from day to day with false hope and unrealistic expectations. This does not benefit you or the family member suffering from schizophrenia.

7) Individual therapy to deal with feelings of despair, guilt, helplessness and anger might be of benefit for family members.

Chapter XXIV

DISRUPTIVE BEHAVIOR DISORDERS OF CHILDHOOD AND ADOLESCENCE

Conduct Disorder and Oppositional Defiant Disorder

Wwe have discussed a number of problems and disorders which usually begin in childhood or adolescence. These include attention deficit disorder, bulimia, anorexia and adolescent drug abuse and dependency. In the following chapters we will explore anxiety disorders of childhood and adolescence and depression. This chapter is devoted to a discussion of disruptive behaviors—specifically conduct disorders. Attention deficit hyperactivity disorder is also classified as a disruptive behavior disorder. Parents and teachers of children suffering from ADHD can testify as to the validity of including ADHD in this category of disorders. (Refer to Chapter XI.)

DSM IV makes a distinction between conduct disorder where the rights of others are violated and oppositional defiant disorder where the child or adolescent is negative, hostile and defiant but does not violate the rights of others. There is also a classification of conduct disorder called adjustment disorder with disturbance of conduct. This is where an identifiable stressor is present. An example of this may be acting out behaviors following the death of a parent or a divorce. Children and adolescents often act out their feelings in such instances. They also tend to act out their depression. This will be discussed in the chapter on depression in children and adolescents.

Conduct disorder behaviors may take place with others, in which case it is classified as "group type" or be initiated by the individual alone. This is identified as "solidary aggressive type." There is also a residual class called disruptive behavior disorders with a mixture of behaviors not otherwise specified. In order to be classified as a conduct disorder the disruptive behaviors must have persisted for at least six months. At least three of the following behaviors must be present.

1) Stealing without confrontation of the victim
2) Running away from home
3) Lying
4) Fire setting
5) Truancy
6) Breaking and entry
7) Destroying property of another individual
8) Physical cruelty to animals
9) Use of a weapon more than one time in a fight
10) Initiation of fights frequently
11) Stealing with confrontation
12) Physical cruelty to others
13) Staying out at night
14) Intimidating others

The disorder is classified as mild, moderate or severe and is described as childhood onset or adolescent onset.

Oppositional defiant disorder is the diagnosis in cases of disturbances (more frequent than normal) including:

1) Loss of temper
2) Arguing with adults
3) Defiance of adults
4) Annoying others
5) Blaming others for their own mistakes
6) Irritability and frequent anger and resentment
7) Vindictiveness

The essential feature in conduct disorders is a persistent pattern of behaviors which violate the rights of others. This behavior can take place at home, at school or in the community. As the behaviors continue unchecked, there is a tendency for escalation. At later ages physical violence may take place including rape or assault. There is a tendency to develop antisocial attitudes and behaviors.

Associated features include use of alcohol and mood altering drugs, school failure, gang membership and lack of remorse, guilt or concern for the welfare of others. Low self-esteem and a sense of failure is common with compensatory ego defense of bravado and grandiosity. Beneath this facade are often feelings of depression and anxiety. In fact, major depression is, in many cases, the primary diagnosis with conduct disorder secondary. Depression in adolescents will be discussed in a following chapter.

Individuals suffering from learning disabilities and attention deficit hyperactivity disorder are more prone to become depressed as well as act out their emotions than the general population. Individuals with ADHD are often labelled as behavior problems. Often their inattention and impulsivity is considered to be voluntary. Teachers and parents commonly do not realize that these are symptoms of ADHD and not volitional. Conflict between child and parent and child and teacher soon develops. Rather than treating the ADHD disorder, the relationship becomes one of control. The child or adolescent usually becomes frustrated and rebellious. Feelings of failure and depression are not uncommon. As the conflict escalates there is a tendency to act out. Association with others who rebel and use of mood altering drugs leads to more extreme antisocial behaviors and feelings of rejection and alienation from mainstream society.

Individuals from a dysfunctional family are also more likely to develop conduct disorder and oppositional defiant disorder traits and tendencies. Homes in which there is abuse tend to produce angry, rebellious, oppositional individuals. Overindulgent parents raise children who have problems in fitting into society. The children are often non-conforming and self-indulgent, and lack human compassion and empathy. Children raised in an environment that lacks structure or consistency tend to grow up confused as to expectations and appropriate social behaviors. If they have been able to manipulate and split parents as children, they often attempt the same manipulations as adults. This, of course, results in poor interpersonal relationships and problems with intimacy.

Much has been written about children who grow up in alcoholic homes. Acting out behaviors are not uncommon. In some cases conduct disorder behaviors come from frustration and anger. In other cases it is probable that the adolescent is attempting to get help for the family. Family systems theorists suggest that the adolescent is the "scapegoat." In other situations of conduct disorder the adolescent has not developed an internalized sense of self-control possibly because of lack of structure and appropriate discipline at home or lack of adequate role models. Many adolescents do not know how to deal in appropriate and functional ways with negative emotions and situations which cause dysphoria.

More males than females suffer from conduct disorder. This is probably because females in our society have been taught not to become angry or at least not display signs of anger. Men can become angry but not depressed. Men must "defend" and cope but are not allowed to cry. Women must be "lady like" and not act in violent ways. Of course, much of this is changing with violence on T.V. Many of the videos watched by our children and the T.V. shows display antisocial behaviors by males as well as females. Emotional and impulse control does not appear to be a virtue or even acceptable in situations where one's rights have been violated. And, of course, the antisocial adolescent (and adult) finds many instances in their lives which they justify as causal factors in their rage. This appears to be the age of self-indulgence, guns and violence. Unless we make major changes in our society and the way we raise and parent our children, we can expect more and more adolescent Conduct Disorder problems.

The following chapter discusses parenting skills and how a parent can help an adolescent reach adulthood in as healthy a state as possible, emotionally and psychologically. These steps and effective parenting techniques apply to most situations however are especially significant in cases of conduct disorder, drug abuse and other disruptive and dysfunctional adolescent situations.

Chapter XXV

EFFECTIVE PARENTING SKILLS

In the past twenty or thirty years psychology has focused on psychosocial development in an attempt to better understand human behavior. Freud's approach stressed a biological basis to human behavior. Erik Erikson's contribution to understanding our behaviors, attitudes and emotions was based on the premise that we are social "animals" and that we live and grow in a social environment and atmosphere which influences our development and ultimately the way we live, think and feel. Understanding the developmental process gives us, as individuals, a better concept of ourselves as well as others. This helps us in our relationships and in how we view the world. These stages will be discussed briefly in this chapter as an introduction to the section on effective parenting skills. Erikson stressed the idea that at each stage of development there may be problems and that individuals who do not accomplish the "tasks" of a stage may develop emotional problems. This theme will be expanded on to include stressors that may arise at each stage in order for you to more fully understand the particular psychosocial stresses your child or adolescent is experiencing. Hopefully, this will help you respond in an appropriate and healthy way not only for the benefit of the family member but for your own welfare.

While many of the effective parenting principles apply to family life in general, such as open communication techniques, unity in parenting, and providing structure, we will emphasize parenting skills with adolescents in particular.

Erikson suggested that there are eight stages or phases in the life cycle and that development is never completed. According to Erikson's theory, individuals who are not successful in passing from one stage to another and who have not accomplished the related "tasks" in a stage, are burdened with emotional and psychological problems in life. For example, it is hypothesized that an individual who did not develop trust as a child will have problems trusting others in adulthood thus creating problems in intimacy as well as interpersonal relationships. Eriksonian therapists suggest that paranoid, avoidant and narcissistic personality disorders may be related to lack of trust. Certainly there is evidence that personality traits and characteristics begin developing at an early age. It is essential that parents realize this.

Erikson's first stage of psychosocial development is trust vs mistrust. The development of trust occurs as the result of maternal nurturing provided consistently with continuity. The infant learns to trust and rely on others and develops an attitude of hope. Without this, fears of abandonment arise and a sense of separation. As a parent, it is necessary to provide love and nurturance on a consistent basis. This is not very different from the need for positive personal regard, encouragement, and support needed by older children and adolescents. Often parents forget that this need continues.

The second stage of development following early infancy is that of autonomy vs shame and doubt. During this stage the child learns expectations and obligations. There is a demand for self-control and acceptance of authority. Many children who have been spoiled without being expected to follow rules become self-indulgent as adults. Erikson states that such individuals tend to be secretive, manipulative and sly and that these traits are related to lack of acceptance of social rules and obligations. It is suggested that individuals who do not develop a sense of self-control often become antisocial. During this stage of development parents must provide direction and structure, and guide the child in making right choices (the key word is "guide"). This guidance is provided by example as well as setting limits and rules. Again, this type of parenting is required when dealing with adolescents as well as older children.

The third stage is that of initiative. During this stage the child develops a determination for achieving goals and makes plans. The major activity is play and children should be encouraged to experience different tasks, explore, and be allowed to fail. This is a time of the development of a sense of creativity and imagination. Failure to complete this stage results in feelings of guilt. Adolescents need opportunity for success and the chance to fail. Children (as well as adolescents) who are not encouraged to be independent to some extent develop anxieties and fears. Dependent personality disorders and anxiety disorders appear to be related to fixation in this stage of development.

The fourth stage is that of industry vs inferiority. During this stage the individual is faced with the task of controlling impulses and emotions and focusing on accomplishment. The child learns that diligence and persistence pays off. Many adolescents live in a dream world. They do not realize or accept the fact that they need to develop skills and resources for the future. Responsibility is often postponed until well into adulthood. The focus is on joy, freedom and happiness. Drugs often provide temporary relief. These individuals never develop the virtue of competency and the realization that accomplishment results in a sense of pride and self-value. These are the individuals who are often depressed. They deny reality and blame society and others (especially their parents) for not providing support and "not understanding." They tend to be dependent on family and are often antisocial. They expect others to satisfy their needs without reciprocity. During this stage parents are wise to provide positive reinforcement and to help the child face challenges. Encouragement to complete tasks is primary. Adolescents need this direction and encouragement also. Setting unrealistic goals, or requiring the adolescent to become involved in activities which are distasteful from a personal standpoint, should be avoided. It is necessary for the parent to help a youngster realistically assess their resources, skills, and interests and be true to themselves.

The fifth stage is that of identity vs identity confusion. The first four stages are preadolescent stages. This stage is one that takes one from childhood to adulthood and is related to issues of separation, individuation, emancipation and independence vs dependence. During this period the individual is preparing to enter the adult world. It is a time when one is attempting to define moral issues and to develop a value system of their own. External stresses and pressures tend to complicate the process. This is a time of physical change and development. Often there is a sense of awkwardness and confusion. Sexual thoughts become more pervasive and sexual urges more compelling. There is a need to be accepted by others and the danger of negative peer influence. Belonging to a group (or gang) is a part of the peer acceptance process. The fear of rejection may lead to compromised behaviors. Family conflict often arises due to differences of opinion as to what is acceptable and what is not. School problems often develop, especially in cases of undiagnosed speech, language and learning deficits or attention deficit disorder. Stress can often result in psychological problems including depression, anxiety, mood swings and low self-esteem. Often adolescents develop somatic problems such as stomachaches, headaches, hypertension, ulcers and fatigue. Sleep and appetite disturbances are common. Substance abuse may develop from peer pressure or the desire to escape and "feel better." Adolescents are often irritable, insecure and have feelings of hopelessness and failure. Parents can help by being available. Just listening often helps. Too often giving advice creates problems. Remember, adolescents are dealing with issues of autonomy, identity and individuation. Being non-judgemental and non-directive is a proven therapeutic technique. This does not mean that boundaries should not be set and limitations provided. However, it does mean allowing the adolescent to make many decisions on their own when there are no major threats or risks. They may make mistakes but this is necessary in the development of their own life style and identity. Freedom to make an error results in improved judgement ultimately.

This chapter has focused on the first five stages of psychosocial development and pathology which may result from lack of task accomplishment during each stage. It must be emphasized that the stages are not passed through and the gains (or failures) necessarily permanent. It is possible, for example, to regress, especially in cases of stress or trauma. We may, as individuals, lose sight of self and our identity. We may lose trust. This is why I have emphasized the adolescent's need for continued support, reinforcement, understanding, direction and nurturance. Adolescence is, indeed, a time of stress both for the individual and the family. These stressors may be related to identity issues; however there are sometimes other stressors in the family. Many marriages dissolve as the last child leaves home. There may also be financial stressors. The death of a grandparent has been identified as a significant psychosocial stressor during adolescence.

The suggestions made in the text as related to the first five stages of development are appropriate during the entire cycle of parenting. In review they include:

1) Continuity and consistency in parenting. Parents must present a unified front even if they are divorced. This allows for the child or adolescent to feel that there is stability. Parents are often surprised when adolescents admit that they want structure and rules.
2) Provide structure and rules.
3) Provide positive reinforcement, love and respect.
4) Help the child/adolescent explore possibilities and potential. Allow for experimentation and opportunities for success. Allow individuals to be true to themselves and their own interests. Give them the chance to fail and to learn from this failure.
5) As the individual grows, review and restate obligations, expectations and responsibilities, allowing for input from the child. Con-

tracts are often helpful in dealing with older children. Be sure the child understands. Keep rules simple and direct. Allow for self-determination when possible.

6) Encourage the child to seek new challenges. Stress task completion.

7) Help the individual evaluate resources and abilities and make realistic goals and plans. Facilitate and emphasize education. In the case of suspected speech, learning or language deficits or attention deficit disorder get a professional evaluation and develop a remedial plan as soon as possible.

8) Do not involve the child in marital conflicts or problems.

9) Be available to listen. A special time might be set aside. Some parents have discovered that taking a child out for dinner once a week (where the child cannot escape) provides an opportunity to discuss problems and feelings.

10) Use "I messages" rather than "you messages." I messages are non-confrontational and usually result in a win-win situation. The I message is one in which you describe the event and your feelings. For example, "You missed curfew last night and I was angry and worried." You messages add expectations and requirements. These can be added later if the adolescent does not respond in a positive way. Usually the I message results in a conversation which is not as emotional, with resolution of the problem.

11) Share your feelings, needs, goals and life with your child.

12) Allow the child or adolescent to feel negative emotions and then help them develop coping skills. It does not help to tell an adolescent that they should not be angry, sad and upset, for example, if they were not invited to a party. Let them ventilate. Of course it hurts. Then allow the child or adolescent to explore different ways of responding.

13) Face the fact that children grow up and leave. Be realistic about your feelings and plan for the future. Discuss these issues within the family.

14) Seek professional advice if the child or adolescent is abusing drugs or shows signs of emotional problems.

15) Express your pride and joy in your children and give thanks for the opportunity of guiding and directing them into a happy, healthy, fulfilling adulthood.

The last three stages of development will be discussed in a following chapter. These stages are adult stages.

Chapter XXVI

ANXIETY DISORDERS OF
CHILDHOOD OR ADOLESCENCE

Children and adolescents suffer from anxiety the same as adults. In fact, there is some evidence that the incidence of anxiety disorders among children and adolescents is increasing due to changes in our society and the way we live and parent. Two parent families are not as common, of course, as in the past. Often both parents work. Parenting tasks are taken over by individuals other than the parents. There appears to be a breakdown in the moral fiber of society. Mood altering drugs are more available and gangs more powerful and prevalent. Economic conditions have caused many corporations to cut back in employment, and, for the first time in history, these cut backs are being made in middle management jobs. Individuals who might be saving money to educate their children now are concerned about their own financial security and tomorrow's expenses. There appear to be a lack of feelings of security. This general sense of insecurity and uncertainty impacts on the health of the family as well as the community and society as a whole. Children respond to psychosocial stressors in many ways.

Anxiety disorders of adolescence and childhood include separation anxiety disorder, avoidant disorder and overanxious disorder. (Overanxious disorder in childhood is considered a generalized anxiety disorder in *DSM IV*. Avoidant disorder is included in the *DSM IV* as social phobia.) The specific symptoms of separation anxiety disorder include unrealistic worry of harm to major attachment figures or fear that they will not return; fear of a calamitous event taking place, such as being murdered or kidnapped; reluctance or refusal to go to school with fear of separation or reluctance of going to sleep; avoidance of being alone with clinging or shadowing caretakers; nightmares of separation; somatic complaints to avoid leaving home; temper tantrums if separated; and excessive distress with separation. Distress may be to the point of panic. Fear of the dark is often an associated feature. Individuals suffering from separation anxiety are frequently depressed. They also tend to be in need of constant attention. When there is no demand for separation, the child or adolescent does not typically have problems.

Onset is usually prior to adolescence and often during the preschool years. The disorder varies in degree of intensity and course. There may be periods of remission. Impairment can be severe and cause real problems in the family. Often parents differ on the approach to take with the child, which can cause marital conflict. Parents also tend to become frustrated and anxious themselves. Often they ask the question, "What am I doing wrong?" In this day and age when social skills and social involvement are stressed, parents worry about their child's future even when they are small. The same concerns are present in the case of avoidant disorder of childhood or adolescence.

While there are no specific predisposing personality factors in separation anxiety disorder, the symptoms commonly arise after a particular stressor such as the death of a relative or pet, an illness, a change in the family such as a divorce, or a move to a different school district or neighborhood. Children with the disorder tend to have a close family as opposed to children from homes in which there is neglect.

The primary symptom of avoidant disorder of childhood or social phobia is excessive shrinking from contact with unfamiliar people, which causes impaired social functioning with peers. The individual with this disorder is able to develop and maintain satisfactory relationships with family and well known peers but displays signs of anxiety when required to make contact with others than close friends and family. This disorder usually develops during early school years, however can be developed as early as age two. This is known as "stranger anxiety." The disorder may be episodic, elicited by certain situations and circumstances, or chronic with no identifiable stressor present. It can continue for a long time or improve spontaneously. Impairment may be very severe and result in the development of limited social skills and ability which makes separation, individuation, and independence from family difficult. The disorder is more prevalent among females than males.

The third anxiety disorder of childhood or adolescence is overanxious disorder. This is unrealistic anxiety or worry. As in the case of social phobia, the symptoms must have lasted for at least six months. Worry and concern can be about the future, concern about past behaviors, concern about competency or developing physical illnesses, marked self-consciousness, a need for reassurance or inability to relax. Impairment can be severe. Predisposing factors include birth order (the oldest child), children from upper socioeconomic families, and family demands for achievement by the child or adolescent. The disorder is fairly common and equal in prevalence in males and females. Children of mothers suffering from anxiety disorder tend to develop the disorder more readily than that of the general population. Children suffering from the disorder frequently focus on one particular person as a cause of their problem such as one teacher or a particular neighbor. School and simple phobia are often coexistent. Individuals suffering from overanxious disorder also tend to be perfectionists and may have obsessive compulsive traits. Nail biting and hair pulling are commonly associated features. Onset can be gradual or sudden. It may continue into adult life as an anxiety disorder. Somatic concerns and complaints are common with this disorder and often result in unnecessary medical exams.

A child who is emotionally immature is particularly vulnerable to anxiety. In cases of healthy development and maturation, children tend to handle stress and stressors because they learn coping mechanisms and techniques. They also develop a sense of self and have more confidence and feel more secure. These feelings are more easily developed in an atmosphere of love, attention and nurturance. However, the home atmosphere must also be one which stresses and rewards independence and responsibility. At all stages of development there should be opportunities as well as encouragement to separate. The infant is allowed to explore the environment and separate from the mother figure just as the adolescent should be encouraged to become more independent.

In a healthy, functional family the child or adolescent emancipates and develops a sense of identity different from the family and parents. In healthy separation the outer world becomes important. In unhealthy development the child remains dependent and tends to cling to significant others because of lack of self-confidence and internalized fears. These fears are often fears of abandonment, harm, or rejection. Because individuals in a dysfunctional family have not been made to feel secure, they tend to mistrust others and to live a life of anxiety.

Treatment of separation anxiety begins by identifying the basis of the individual's fear and then encouraging the child to talk about the phobic object. Drawing pictures about the fear and telling stories is one way to help the child visualize his or her fears. Identifying specific fears then allows for a gradual desensitization process. Behavior modification techniques can also be used where the child is exposed to the phobic situation or object accompanied by the parent. Throughout the process it is important that the child be provided with consistent love and made to feel secure. Preparation for a change such as a geographical move should be made in advance. The child should be told also of such things as an operation or anticipated family stressor and be encouraged to discuss their feelings and how such an event will impact on them. Cooperation between the parent, teacher and therapist is primary in the case of school anxiety.

Children and adolescents suffering from avoidant disorder, where they fear relationships outside of the family, are best treated by helping them increase assertiveness. Reward and positive reinforcement are helpful in shaping behavior. Once the individual has experienced some success in the area of social ability and being accepted by others, assertiveness tends to grow. The child should discuss special areas of interest and be provided with opportunities for success. Joining a high school computer club or becoming involved in a noncompetitive activity like art or photography often allows the child or adolescent to become more confident and less shy.

Individuals suffering from overanxious disorder tend to be hard working and ingratiating. They often have a need for perfection and achievement but tend to become easily discouraged. They also tend to fear rejection. It is important that parents provide approval and consistency. In therapy the child or adolescent should be encouraged to talk about the need for excellence and to develop realistic goals and values. Sibling rivalry should also be discussed with the parents emphasizing the fact that individuals differ in their abilities and resources and must take their own path to happiness and success rather than competing with others. In the case of overconcern about physical well being, a complete medical exam is suggested. If the results are normal this should be discussed in therapy. Of course, if there are medical problems they should be treated. Vague, non-specific physical complaints tend to be symptomatic of anxiety.

Chapter XXVII

ADOLESCENT AND CHILDHOOD
DEPRESSION AND SUICIDE

Just as adolescents and children can develop anxiety disorders, they can become clinically depressed. While children and adolescents react differently, there are many commonalities in the symptoms of their depressions as well as the causes. Stress within the family, such as death, financial problems or marital conflict impact on all of the family members. Of course, each responds differently, depending on their emotional make-up and abilities. However, psychosocial stressors often create anxiety as well as depression.

Developmental factors including separation from family and developing a sense of initiative and industry create stress in children. Issues of identity and peer acceptance; physiological changes; and preparing for the future can be overwhelming and create feelings of depression in adolescents. Children with attention deficit disorder and speech, language, and learning disorders are especially prone to depression. They often feel inadequate and develop a failure identity. Academic problems tend to increase in middle school and high school when verbal skills become more important. Family conflict develops because of lack of achievement and poor performance exacerbating the depression experienced by the child or adolescent.

Type "A" children are also prone to depression. These are the individuals who strive for super success and achievement. They are the class stars or the star athletes who tend to overachieve and be perfectionists. Anxiety disorders as well as depression are common. Girls are likely to develop problems with physical image and eating disorder symptoms are not uncommon.

Emotionally immature children and the overprotected child may have problems separating from the significant caretaker and are also predisposed for depression, especially when required to leave the safety and security of home.

Adolescents who use and abuse mood altering drugs are often depressed. This can be primary when drugs are used to self-medicate. In other cases, there may be other causes for the depression such as an endogenous factor. Or the depression can be secondary in which case the drugs increase the symptoms of depression. In either situation mood altering drugs tend to increase mood swings and problems in school and at home.

Because children and adolescents commonly have not developed the ability to get in touch with their feelings and often have problems talking to adults, their depression usually goes unnoticed. In most cases childhood and adolescent depression begins with feelings of confusion and dysphoria. During this stage, the individual experiences a number of different feelings, most of them negative. They may feel uncomfortable in social situations, or they may become irritable, anxious, and tense. Often they begin to act out their depression. They may withdraw and become isolative. Sleep and eating disturbances develop. In cases of internalized depression they may develop feelings of self-hatred, despair, hopelessness and low self-esteem. They may become apathetic and experience anhedonia where they find little joy or satisfaction from activities and situations which were previously enjoyable.

Children and adolescents experiencing depression may speak of suicide. Danger signs include withdrawal, refusal to communicate, a lack of school involvement, a drop in grades, expressions of anger against the parent, somatic problems, crying spells, no plans for the future, giving away personal belongings, and of course, talk of suicide. Suicidal ideations and expressions of a desire to die always should be taken seriously and professional help sought.

Situations and stressors which increase the risk of suicide include use or abuse of drugs, a recent death of a loved one or friend, termination of a relationship with a boyfriend or girlfriend, a recent divorce or change in the living situation, failure in school or disappointment in an important activity or area of interest.

An alarming increase in suicide attempts and suicides among children has taken place over the last years. Some of these children have been preschool age. Because children are often not aware of their feelings, have problems expressing themselves verbally, and tend to think in concrete terms, parents should be especially aware of signs and symptoms of depression.

Suicide is the second leading cause of death among adolescents following traffic deaths. More girls than boys attempt suicide, however, because males tend to use more lethal methods, they are more successful. Adolescents who use and abuse drugs are at a higher risk for suicide than the general adolescent population. Impulsivity and lack of emotional control are also risk factors. Risk tends to run in families. There is a higher risk of child and adolescent suicide if one of the parents suffers from depression and if there is a history of family of origin suicide. Cluster suicides have become more frequent where the suicide of one teenager results in additional suicides.

Children and adolescents have many needs. Meeting these needs or providing for them as a parent can facilitate healthy growth and development. Some of these principles have been discussed already. Children and adolescents need love; room to grow; structure; boundaries and limits; consistency and stability; friends outside the home; opportunities for success and achievement; tradition and family rites; adult role models and adults available to listen and guide and direct them toward their own goals and happiness. Parenting is a big job and a major responsibility. A lack of communication fosters emotional problems throughout the growth period. Needs change; however, being available and not only listening but being honest, direct and open with your own feelings is important. Most problems can be solved within the family, however outside help might be required, especially in situations where the child or adolescent is displaying symptoms of depression and most certainly when he or she talks about committing suicide.

Chapter XXVIII

PERSONALITY DISORDERS

In a previous chapter the first five stages of Erikson's psychosocial development were discussed and how failure to move through these stages may result in psychological and emotional problems. In this chapter we will discuss the last three stages of development. These stages take place beginning in young adulthood. Erikson points out that not everyone moves through all of these stages. Arrestment or fixation at an early level of psychosocial development may take place or an individual may regress.

The sixth stage or phase is intimacy vs isolation. This is the stage during which individuals seek relationships, partnerships and affiliations. It is obvious that unless they trust others and have a sense of identity their needs will not be met. Relationships are not mutually satisfying and rewarding unless partners are committed and able to share and be honest. Individuals who have experienced rejection and abandonment as children or have not had their childhood needs met often attempt to seek these needs in adulthood and in adult relationships. Thus, it is not uncommon to see those who have not received proper nurturing and love carry with them into adulthood feelings of inadequacy lack and low self-esteem. Often these individuals develop compensatory defenses. They are demanding and/or dependent. They need constant attention and reassurance. These people, because of fears of rejection and inadequacy, become histrionic and narcissistic.

Other individuals become avoidant. They have not developed social skills and are overly sensitive to the opinions of others. They do not enter social situations or relationships unless they are assured of acceptance. Passive aggressive individuals tend to have problems with intimacy because they are not assertive. They have not developed a clear image of self and of their needs. Often they lack emotional awareness. This makes intimacy difficult because they do not know who they are or what they need. They try to avoid obligations and responsibility. Here we also see a lack of industry and initiative. Individuals suffering from schizoid personality disorder neither desire nor enjoy close relationships. Lack of the ability to relate to others in a committed intimate way leads to isolation and alienation. This also tends to result in or contribute to feelings of loneliness, alienation, and depression.

The seventh stage of development is generativity vs stagnation. This is a time when the individual focuses on ideas and begins developing guidelines for future generations. Individuals have a sense of caring and sharing. They tend to be generous with themselves and their resources. Fulfillment is achieved by helping others succeed. The joy of teaching others, being a good parent or grandparent, and giving to the community are the rewards of generativity. Being a good and fair leader or supervisor is an example of generativity. An individual who has not reached this stage tends to become stagnated. Rather than teaching and sharing, they become demanding, rigid, and authoritarian. Antisocial personality traits are common as is an egocentric focus and outlook on life. Individuals who are paranoid tend to have problems with generativity and giving to others.

The final stage is integrity vs despair. Individuals who reach this stage reap the benefits from the accomplishments and tasks completed during the first seven stages. They have feelings of order and meaning in their lives. Dignity and sense of security develops because they have developed their own style without condemning others. Individuals who have reached this stage tend to be loving and non-judgemental. Wisdom is their virtue. They continue to see life with interest and curiosity and have feelings of wholeness and completeness. Those who have not reached this stage tend to fear the future. Life is meaningless and there are feelings of despair and anxiety as the aging process continues.

Examining psychosocial developmental stages is just one way of viewing personality disorders. There are many other models and ways of attempting to understand characterological or personality and pathological traits, attitudes, and behaviors which result in dysfunction. It must be emphasized that all of us have some of the traits which will be discussed. In fact, it might be of benefit for you to examine which of the symptoms you yourself display and how these symptoms interfere with your life and your relationships and possible changes you might make.

Personality disorders are enduring behaviors or traits which result in significant impairment in social or occupational functioning or subjective distress. These are not behaviors or traits that are related to episodes of illness although many of the symptoms may be seen during an episode of another mental disorder.

The symptoms are often recognizable during adolescence and tend to become more extreme and fixed in adult life. The impact on family members and significant others varies depending on the disorder and the severity; however, often the behaviors and traits are very disturbing, disruptive, and dysfunctional. Initially a distinction was made between neurosis and pathology. One way of considering personality disorders is that the attitudes and behaviors are indeed neurotic and dysfunctional. Often work is impaired, sometimes because of inability to get along with others. Unless there are other coexisting mental illnesses, hospitalization is usually not required. Individuals with personality disorders do not usually seek treatment.

The personality disorders have been grouped into clusters. Cluster A includes paranoid, schizoid, and schizotypal personality disorder. A common trait is that individuals with any one of these disorders appear odd or eccentric. Cluster B includes antisocial, borderline, histrionic and narcissistic disorders. Those with these disorders are dramatic, emotional or erratic. Cluster C includes avoidant, dependent, and obsessive compulsive personality disorder. Sufferers are anxious or fearful. Living with someone who is odd, eccentric, dramatic, emotional, erratic, anxious or fearful is difficult.

Some discussion has taken place regarding paranoia. Paranoid personality disorder symptoms include expectation of being harmed or exploited, lack of trust of friends and associates, suspicions of being slandered, bearing of grudges, fear of confiding in others, overreacting when slighted, and questioning the fidelity of a sexual partner.

Schizoid personality disorder sufferers are indifferent to social relationships and tend to be cold and aloof. They are loners. Praise and criticism do not effect them. They tend to be aggressive and hostile as well as self-absorbed. Males with this disorder have problems dating and rarely marry. Females tend to be passive. Social relationships are severe. Living with someone who is suffering from paranoid personality disorder or schizoid personality disorder is difficult and usually unsatisfying.

Individuals who are schizotypal tend to have peculiar ideas and often behave and appear odd and strange. They are extremely anxious in social situations. Odd beliefs can include superstitions, belief in mystical powers, and the belief of being controlled by others. Friends are few. Speech is often odd and inappropriately abstract or vague. The individual is also often paranoid. Borderline personality disorder traits are also often present.

Antisocial personality disorder was previously called psychopathic or sociopathic disorder. The essential feature of this disorder is a pattern of irresponsible and antisocial behavior. The corresponding childhood disorder is conduct disorder. Antisocial behaviors are characterized by a lack of regard for the rights of others. Imagine how difficult it would be to be married to someone suffering from this disorder.

This disorder often results in legal problems. Individuals are usually not self-supporting and are more likely than the general population to spend time in jail or die prematurely by violent means. Often they abuse mood altering drugs. Predisposing factors are attention deficit disorder and conduct disorder. The disorder tends to be familial. Three percent of adult males suffer from this disorder, and one percent of adult females. Symptoms include inability to work consistently; acting in unlawful ways; irritability and aggressiveness; failure to honor financial obligations; lying consistently; impulsive acting out; reckless behavior with little regard for one's safety or the safety of others; lack of the ability to be a responsible parent; inability to sustain a monogamous relationship for more than one year; and a lack of remorse. Again, these behaviors create real problems for family members.

Borderline personality disorder is characterized by instability of mood, interpersonal relationships and self-image problems. Individuals often act in impulsive ways with a potential for self-destruction, have radical mood shifts, react with intense anger, threaten suicide, have chronic feelings of emptiness and boredom and have fears of abandonment. Borderline personality disorder sufferers tend to create an atmosphere of anxiety and fear in the family. They may also display paranoid or dissociative symptoms.

Individuals suffering from histrionic personality disorder are emotional and act in ways that demand attention. They are often sexually inappropriate and seductive, overly concerned about their physical appearance, display rapid mood swings, are self-centered, and require immediate satisfaction.

The essential features of narcissistic personality disorders are grandiosity, lack of empathy and hypersensitivity to the evaluation of others. They react with rage to criticism, are often exploitive and preoccupied with fantasies of success, have a sense of entitlement and require constant attention. Family members and significant others tend to be ignored and their needs unmet.

An oversensitivity to the opinion of others, social discomfort and timidity are characteristics of avoidant personality disorder. Individuals with this disorder are easily hurt, have no close friends, avoid social gatherings, are easily embarrassed and or exaggerate risks when confronted with the need to perform outside of the ordinary routine.

Dependent personality disorder is characterized by dependent and submissive behavior. Individuals with this disorder do poorly in jobs that require creativity and independent decision making and thus often hold low level jobs. Agoraphobic behaviors are frequently found among sufferers, as is depression. Chronic childhood or adolescent illnesses are predisposing factors.

Those with obsessive compulsive personality disorder tend to be perfectionists, preoccupied with detail, controlling, workaholics, inflexible, and parsimonious. They usually have problems relaxing and having fun.

Individuals often suffer from more than one personality disorder. Again the level of dysfunction depends on the particular disorder or disorders and the severity of the symptoms.

Family members must realize that individuals suffering from personality disorders usually resist change. Their attitudes and behaviors have developed over a period of time and tend to be well established. Often family members have become accustomed to the symptoms and try to overlook them. A certain amount of tolerance is probably a good idea. However, if the behaviors become burdensome and interfere with your own need fulfillment, happiness and functional ability, you should consider taking action. Just as the spouse or significant other in a relationship with someone who is abusing alcohol or other mood altering drugs must be realistic, an individual in a dysfunctional personal situation or relationship because of personality disorder problems must make an evaluation. Although the family member with the disorder may not seek help, you can, as an individual. Talking to a professional often allows you to make decisions regarding your level of tolerance, needs and how to face the future.

Chapter XXIX

DEVELOPING A STRESS MANAGEMENT PLAN

S tress is the physiological response to the environment which results in increased autonomic system activation. In situations of stress our heart beats more rapidly, we tend to perspire, blood rushes from the extremities to the heart and brain, our eyes dilate and we become generally more alert and vigilant.

These responses have their origin in the fight/flight syndrome and, in days gone by, prepared us to defend or flee in situations of danger. These responses can still be functional in today's emergencies and life situations. The adrenaline pumps and we become alert when confronted with danger. Stories have been told about individuals who have acted with great courage and strength in situations of crisis. However, continued alertness, vigilance and physiological excitement tend to overtax the body systems. Stress, unrelieved, has been connected with a number of physical and medical pathologies and problems including heart disease and hypertension, gastrointestional problems, headaches and even asthma. Unrelieved anxiety and stress can also cause emotional and psychological confusion and chronic fatigue syndrome.

The ability to deal with stress varies with the individual. Some people are able to function under a high level of stress. Others become dysfunctional and respond in neurotic or pathological ways when confronted with stress. A number of the mental and emotional illnesses discussed in this book are, in part at least, related to dysfunctional ways of dealing with stress. Personality disorders such as obsessive compulsive disorder and avoidant personality disorder are examples of how individuals respond in inadequate and unadaptive ways to their environment. Anxiety disorders are another example.

Many people tend to decompensate under stress. Neurotic and pathological responses then become more prevalent. There is also a tendency to regress. This is true not only with children but also with adults. When we believe we "have it all together" and have, in our opinion, reached a state of control, a stressor can cause us to become less functional than we

155

expect and respond in ways which are not adaptive or healthy. A divorce or death often results in unexpected and unwanted responses in family members.

Exposure over a long period of time to stress can result in the gradual diminishing of ego defenses and functional ability. One example of chronic stress is mental illness in the family. Often pathological or nonadaptive responses develop. Living in an alcoholic family results in dysfunctional responses and behaviors developed over time. The spouse of someone who is alcoholic does not suddenly become codependent. Codependent behaviors develop as the relationship continues. Children in an alcoholic home or one in which one of the parents suffer from another form of mental illness tend to have problems. Because these responses and pattern of behaviors have developed over time, they are often difficult to change. Bad habits take time to correct. This is why it is important to develop a stress management plan.

Developing a stress management plan helps the body to prepare for stressors and crisis. A stress management plan also allows one to develop adaptive techniques and attitudes to deal with stress when it arises.

Studies have identified how various events and situations impact on individuals. Of course, each individual adapts or responds differently based on characterological factors and past experiences as well as other factors such as age. Children and adolescents respond differently to stress than adults in that they are dealing with different developmental issues. For example, as discussed, adolescents are more impacted by events and situations that threaten their identity. Not being accepted by others can be traumatic. Adults also vary in their responses based on life situation differences. When an individual has achieved a certain degree of financial success and stability, they may not be as negatively impacted by such things as job loss, although job loss is always a narcissistic injury and insult.

Change is always stressful, even in situations where the change may be positive, such as in the case of a job promotion. The most stressful situations, however, are usually situations of loss, such as the death of a spouse, divorce or sickness.

Research suggests that exposure to stress and stressors can have a cumulative impact on the individual. The impact becomes more severe, for example, when more than one stressful or traumatic event or situation takes place in a short period of time. This is also true in cases where past stressors have not been resolved. For example, some people continue to hold resentments and anger over a long period of time. Individuals who have not resolved emotional problems and issues tend to become more prone to the development of somatic and psychological disorders.

There are ways to protect one's self from the detrimental impact of stress. One way is to develop emotional and ego defense mechanisms. Another is to take care of one's self physically. A healthy body is able to deal with stress in a more adaptive and functional way. A stress management plan with a focus on staying healthy physically includes three components. These components are diet, relaxation and exercise. A proper diet provides the body with the necessary nutrients and elements for good physical health. Certain foods contribute to malfunction. Overindulgence in alcohol, smoking, and too much salt and sugar cannot only lead to physical disease but also have a negative impact on the ability to cope with stress and anxiety.

Exercise is also important in maintaining a healthy body which functions under normal conditions as well as conditions of stress. Exercise is important in metabolism, maintaining body strength and mobility, and controlling weight. Studies have indicated that moderate and regular exercise can improve mood and promote emotional and psychological health.

Relaxation is the third component in a physical wellness and stress management plan. Too few of us know how to relax. Inability to relax results in unresolved tension and anxiety. We often have not developed the attitudes necessary to deal with stress and tension. On vacation we tend to want to "do" rather than "be." We do not take much time in our lives to think, contemplate, enjoy and experience quiet time. As Thoreau wrote "Men lead lives of quiet desperation." We tend to be driven as a nation and as a society. Alcohol and drugs are used to escape. When under pressure or tension we often turn to the world of modern medicine for relief rather than identifying the problem and developing a better way of coping. We want immediate relief. Tranquilizers often appear to be a long term solution when in reality they provide for temporary relief only. Antianxiety medication tends to be addictive and habit forming with individuals becoming physically as well as psychologically dependent on them.

Other forms of dealing with stress may be just as addictive and counterproductive as being dependent on drugs. (Alcohol, incidentally, is a drug.) As a nation we tend to be addicted to T.V. There are also theorists who suggest that we are becoming addicted to violence, sex and external forms of vivid stimulation and excitement. These theorists suggest that we are no longer able to self-stimulate. They state that we have become a nation of spectators rather than being actively involved in life. We want immediate satisfaction and excitement. This is unfortunate because often we have not developed a tolerance for frustration. Healthy management of stress requires that we develop a certain amount of tolerance, patience and understanding. Having a relaxed attitude and feeling in control helps us deal with stress.

Relaxation is not necessarily passive. In developing your own stress management plan try to identify ways to relax that allow you to grow and remain involved. Try new activities and develop more interests. Involve your mind. Do something different. Experiment. Create. Learn. Grow. Activities involving these elements can help you relax as well as handle stress and stressors in a more adaptive and functional way.

We have discussed three basic elements in developing your own stress management plan. These are diet, exercise, and relaxation. Now we will focus on specific techniques in dealing with stress. One of the most important factors in stress management is to become aware of our emotions, especially in relation to how a psychosocial stressor effects us. In this way we can deal directly not only with the stressor but also with emotional responses to the stressor.

Too often we repress our emotions or are in a state of denial. Repressed emotions tend to create tension and anxiety. As a culture we are taught to "handle" stress and crisis. This is especially so in dysfunctional families as discussed in a previous chapter. Therapy might be defined as the art of helping individuals become more aware of their feelings and emotions and then facilitating more adaptive ways to deal with these feelings. It is not "bad" or unnatural to, at times, feel angry, sad, hopeless, helpless, anxious, confused, afraid, depressed, and despondent. The "bad" part is failure to acknowledge these feelings and then make changes in one's life or life situation.

Individuals who deal with stress in a healthy way tend to know how they feel and have allowed themselves the possibility of making changes. Basically, the ability to deal with stress has two components. They are knowledge and power. Knowledge not only of our feelings but also the true nature of the situation and power to make changes, not changes in others but in our attitudes and behaviors.

Knowing how we feel is the first step. For example, in situations of loss individuals are often complimented on how "well" they handled, for example, the death of a loved one. Psychologically, individuals who have lost a loved one are usually, initially, in a state of shock. Just as in the case of a physical injury, the mind tends to shut down. Individuals in grief become emotionally numb and do not experience the loss because, physiologically, they are not able to immediately deal with the loss. However, encouragement to continue denial extends the period of grief and can lead to lack of healthy resolution. The same applies to other situations of stress such as job loss and divorce.

Emotional awareness in dealing with positive change is just as important. A job promotion requires change. There is commonly an element of anxiety, possibly the fear of failure, and often feelings of loss. A job promotion may require moving, and changing friends, and elicit negative family responses.

Identifying stress related feelings and emotions and talking about them tends to relieve the stress. Discussing one's feelings in stress situations with those who are also impacted by the situation is beneficial. Unfortunately, encouraging others to disclose their feelings is almost as forbidden in our culture and society as disclosing our own emotions.

A second principle in managing stress is to analyze the stressor as accurately as possible. This is the intellectual component in managing stress. Being aware of our emotions is not enough. We must be able to identify the problem and then develop ways of solving the problem. Individuals who are successful in managing stress develop techniques to deal with broad ranges of problems and stressors just as successful managers in business have developed problem solving techniques which can be applied to many situations.

Some of these principles and techniques will be discussed. You are encouraged to develop others which are appropriate to your own life style, personality, and situation. There are a number of excellent books and articles on various stress management techniques.

One technique might be referred to as "time framing." Time framing is a cognitive technique. Cognition is the manner or way in which we view the world around us. The way we view the world effects our attitudes and behaviors. Thoughts also effect our emotions. When we see the world as threatening, punitive and dangerous, we become anxious and even paranoid. If we look for the positive elements in people and situations we tend to become less defensive and find more pleasure in situations and relationships.

Time framing is a way of viewing situations and circumstances which provides us with a better perspective and allows us to improve reality testing. It is a way of protecting us from over reacting in situations of stress. The way to use this technique is to ask how important a stressful event or situation will be to us in the future. For example, being delayed in traffic for a period of time is not only frustrating and irritating but also produces stress. We tend to be in a hurry and place deadlines on ourselves. Any delay causes us to feel as if we do not have control of the situation. Delays such as this tend to disturb individuals who are perfectionists or obsessive compulsive more than others. The longer the delay the more likely we are to become upset.

When we ask ourselves how significant or important a delay will be to us in a week or month or a year we gain a better perspective. Of course, the more stressful the event the longer and greater the impact. The loss of a job will matter in a week or month but maybe not in a year. Take time to time-frame irritable, stressful, and disturbing events and situations, and it is likely that you will not overreact in the future.

Another way to minimize stress is a technique called "prepare and prevent." In situations of anticipated stress we can prepare ourselves so that the stress is less likely to have a major impact on us. Preparing for a move by visiting the area prior to the date of departure helps prepare for the event and makes it seem less abrupt. It might be wise to stay in the location for a week or long weekend and explore the stores, the parks and the town. Locating a grocery store, a hardware store and a physician helps prepare for the change. In the case of a family move the children should be included.

Some stressors can be prepared for in advance. Others can be prevented. Too often we believe that we are the victims of chance. Adequate preparation can sometimes prevent catastrophe. Car problems on a vacation can pretty well be prevented by having the car inspected and serviced. Major illness often can be prevented by having an annual examination and following healthy living habits. These are some ways of reducing the risk of a stressor taking place by taking preventative action.

Taking control is another way of dealing with stress. When we feel that we do not have power to change things we tend to become victims and fail to utilize the abilities and resources which we have. Power comes from having choices. In a situation of stress list all of the choices which you have as well as the best possible outcome and the worst. Expect the best outcome but prepare for the worst by giving yourself options. If you lose your job you may have to take a position which is temporarily less prestigious or pays less money, however this is an option. Other options include changing careers or location, going back to school or developing new skills. A crisis can be defined as having two components—trauma and opportunity. Developing different options provides one with power and decreases feelings of helplessness.

Another technique for dealing with stress is, in effect, opposite of the above suggestion which is to take power and act. Some situations require detachment. Under stress there is a tendency to react immediately. These reactions can be irrational and emotional. Doing nothing can result in a better perspective. Compromises and negotiations often come with time. Unsatisfactory relationships may improve when there is no pressure to make immediate changes. Feelings of resentment, anger and hurt may become less severe and extreme. Children and adolescents with behavior problems are often encouraged to take a "time out." In dealing with stress, a "time out" can be beneficial.

One way of detaching and taking a "time out" is to become involved in other activities and develop new interests. Individuals who are experiencing marital problems, for example, can become obsessed with the situation. They tend to overanalyze the remarks and behaviors of the spouse. Detaching and becoming involved in activities not related to the marriage can allow for an improved perspective. In times of stress we do not always need immediate solutions.

Another stress reduction technique is the "Oh Well," "So What," "Who Cares?" response. Taken to extremes, of course, this can result in many problems. However, often we are overly sensitive to the opinions of others and too conscientious for our own welfare. There are many times when it might be healthy and beneficial to say, "Oh, Well," "So What" and "Who Cares?"

Meditation is another way of providing relief from stress. Taking a time each day to be quiet is a form of focusing. Answers often come in quiet times when we are not pushing for solutions. During these times it might be of benefit to define our personal needs and goals. Too often we have lost sight of the direction of our lives, what we want and what makes us happy. Defining needs helps us regain feelings of power as well as identity because we can then take steps to satisfy our needs. One technique is to list the five most important needs in your life. Needs differ. Everyone has different needs. Some people need to be loved. Others need to give love. Some people need to be respected. Achievement, material success, caring for someone, or being respected as a leader are all needs.

One of the problems which we tend to have in life and which leads to stress is that often we believe that all of our needs must be met, for example, in a marriage or a relationship. This results in a stressful situation for both people. Expectations are too high with a probability for failure. Needs can be met in the work place, in the family, and in the community as well as in a relationship. Realizing this and arranging to have these needs met outside of a marriage or relationship is healthy and reduces stress. A high power business executive may have his or her need for control, power, and respect met on the job. He or she does not have to control and terrorize the family. Nursing or medicine may provide for satisfaction of the need to care for others. This individual thus does not have to be codependent in a relationship. If your needs are not being met look for new ways in different areas where these needs can be met.

Another way of coping with stress is role rehearsal. This is a form of preparation. Rehearsing how you will behave in a stressful situation can provide you with insight as to possibilities and methods which can result in a positive outcome. For example, if you are required to appear in court, rehearse your role. Start by imagining the setting, the scene and the circumstance. How would you like to appear and act? Choose a hero and determine how your hero would respond. Once you have a hero you can explore ideal behaviors and attitudes as opposed to real behaviors and attitudes and make adjustments in your future acts and thoughts.

These are just a few techniques which can be used in reducing stress. Remember, you have the power to change the impact of a stressor on yourself by deciding how you are going to respond and react.

Chapter XXX

TREATMENT APPROACHES

The first step in the treatment of mental illness is to obtain a valid diagnosis. Unfortunately treatment often begins without a diagnosis. This is like taking a trip without knowing where one is going or without having a destination. To often medication is prescribed without knowing what is wrong based on the demand for immediate cure and relief. In other cases, psychotherapists treat the symptoms but not the underlying causal factors. Of course, in both of these cases, relief is temporary. More will be said about diagnostic techniques and methods in the following chapter.

Another problematic factor in the treatment of mental illness, in addition to either the lack of a diagnosis or a diagnosis which is not accurate, is resistance to treatment. Society appears to accept the fact that people become physically ill; however, there continues to be a stigma attached to emotional and psychological problems. While this is changing, due to the efforts of the mental health profession and a more understanding and open attitude on the part of the general population, individuals who are suffering from mental illness tend to deny and resist treatment. The postponement of treatment can not only result in increased symptoms and pathology but also extend suffering and dysfunction for the individual and significant others. As was discussed, one of the most useful approaches which can be taken by family members is to help the individual accept the fact that they need help.

Basically there are two forms of treatment for mental illness. One is called organic therapy and focuses on organic or physical causes or pathology. The most commonly organic therapies use mood altering drugs although acupuncture, hemodialysis, orthomolecular therapy (where large dosages of Niacin are prescribed), and electrotherapy have been used in the past. Drugs used in an attempt to control or cure mental illness are called psychotropic drugs.

The second approach in treating mental illness focuses on mediation or changing attitudes and behaviors. This is based on the theory that emotions are the result of thought processes and that changes in the way an individual views the world and conceptualizes his role in the world can improve adaptive and functional ability.

Some of those who espouse organic treatment report that use of mood altering drugs is primary and in some cases the only intervention required. This may be true in some cases of pathology although behavioral and functional problems often develop in conjunction with illnesses whose cause may be organic. Individuals who are suffering from schizophrenia tend to be isolated and alienated from the mainstream. As has been discussed at length, individuals with mental illnesses usually have problems in major life situation areas including relationships, career and social interactions. Studies indicate that most behavioral and characterological disorders cannot be treated solely with psychotropic drugs. Psychotropic drugs also have side effects. Psychotropic medication, according to recent studies, must be used with caution, especially with the elderly and those who are physically ill. Side effects and therapeutic responses must be monitored on a regular basis. This will be discussed in the following chapter. It is suggested that if therapy includes the use of mood altering drugs the patient should insist that arrangements are made for regular supervision and reevaluation as to the need. This is especially true in the case of drugs which can cause dependence such as antianxiety medication and antipsychotic drugs which can cause irreversible Parkinson-like symptoms such as tremors, stiffness, muscle spasms, agitation and restless.

There is also the chance, in using drugs alone, that the basic underlying cause may not be treated such as in the case of grief. Resolution of loss and grief is a psychological process. In many cases, a combination of organic and psychotherapy intervention is of benefit.

Science has made gains in treating mental illness with the basic breakthrough occurring in the mid 1950's. At that time there were over 500,000 patients in mental hospitals. It was estimated that in 20 more years the psychiatric population would reach 800,000. Psychiatric hospitals were portrayed as zoos and "snake pits" often with justification. The patients were violent in many cases and hope of discharge and improvement was poor.

In the late 1950's Thorazine was introduced to treat schizophrenia with dramatic results. Thorazine (a neuroleptic drug) is not a cure for schizophrenia, but it does alleviate the most severe psychotic symptoms and has resulted in a dramatic decrease in the number of patients who must be hospitalized. Since that time a number of other neuroleptic drugs have been introduced. The major improvement in this form of medication is a reduction in the risk of the development of irreversible side effects. Also, antiparkinsonian medication can be given concurrently with neuroleptic medication to reduce risk.

Antidepressants are another type of psychotropic drug. These drugs are used for endogenous depression where there appears to be problems related to neurotransmitter functioning. However, antidepressant medications do not seem to be very beneficial in cases of exogenous depression. Exogenous depression is caused by situational factors such as loss or death. Antidepressant medication can improve mood temporarily but does not change personality characteristics permanently. For individuals with severe, chronic depression or those where psychotropic medication is counterindicated, such as during pregnancy, electroconvulsive therapy is still used on occasion. ECT provides more immediate response whereas antidepressant medication tends to take four to six weeks to reach a therapeutic level. In the case of risk of suicide where the individual cannot be hospitalized, ECT might also be considered. The primary side effect of ECT is memory loss which may be permanent.

Bipolar or manic depressive disorder is treated effectively with Lithium. Medical compliance is often resisted however with patients complaining of side effects. There can also be damage to the liver and kidneys. Monitoring of the blood level plus occasional "drug holidays" are commonly used.

Antianxiety medications are the most commonly prescribed and the most commonly abused psychotropic drugs. There is the risk of dependence. Withdrawal can create severe problems. Reliance on antianxiety medication tends to result in the individual not developing and maintaining adequate coping and functional skills. When used with elderly or demented patients, there is a risk of toxicity. Antianxiety medication can cloud sensorium, impair memory and increase sedation in the elderly. Developing ways to cope with stress and anxiety appear to be more beneficial than medicating for relief of the symptoms only.

Sedative hypnotics have also been used to treat anxiety. With these drugs there is the risk of overdose. They too have a high potential for abuse and addiction.

Psychotropic drugs have been used recently to treat chemical dependency. The results appear to be mixed. Many drug treatment experts object to treating drug abuse and dependence with other drugs. However, antianxiety medications have been used successfully to diminish withdrawal symptoms. Disulfiram (Antabuse) has also been used to change drinking habits. Ingestion of alcohol with Antabuse creates severe physiological responses including problems with breathing, headache, chest pain and vomiting. It cannot be used by individuals with cardiovascular problems because of risk of heart attack. Antabuse is not a cure for alcoholism in that changes in behavior are required.

The purpose of psychotherapy is to change unhealthy ways in which the individual thinks (attitudes) and acts (behaviors). The approaches to helping the individual make these changes varies according to various theories. Freud suggested that emotional problems resulted from repressed or unconscious sexual and aggressive urges. He believed that failure to acknowledge and sublimate these urges resulted in medical and physical problems. He called these Conversion Disorders. Many contemporary theorists believe that somatic problems are directly related to unresolved emotional problems and issues. Freud's therapeutic approach was to bring these urges and desires to conscious mind and "work through" them. The process was one of abreaction and catharsis. Psychodynamics therapy was the process and took place over a period of years, with sessions as often as five times a week. A modified form of this therapy is still used.

Carl Jung added another element in the attempt to understand human behavior. He believed that there was a "collective unconscious" that influenced people. In other words, the thoughts and images of a culture are important determinants in how we feel and think. Both Jung and Freud used dream analysis to help the individual gain insight as to their beliefs and motivations.

Erik Erikson added a social element and emphasized developmental phases and tasks in an attempt to explain attitudes and behaviors. Eriksonian therapists attempt to reeducate individuals who have become fixated at one or another stage. This has been discussed earlier.

Social therapy or psychology places the emphasis on interpersonal relationships. The focus in interpersonal psychotherapy is to improve social abilities and help individuals relate in more adaptive and functional ways. Communication methods are commonly examined and explored with an emphasis on direct and assertive ways of expressing one's self. Better receptive language or listening skills are also discussed.

Family systems therapy focuses on the family as a unit and analyzes roles, rules, and rituals. Some of these have been discussed in a previous chapter. Unhealthy roles and interpersonal interactions in the family are examined with the goal of making changes. Marital therapy also focuses on interactions and roles as well as needs and how these needs may or may not be met in a marriage or relationship.

Behavior modification therapy is focused primarily on changing behaviors rather than attitudes or the way we think. Behavioralists believe that the way we act in the present is related to past experiences. Behaviors which were developed and reinforced in earlier times, unless extinguished, continue to be used by the individual in an attempt to satisfy needs. Of course, in many cases these behaviors, habits, and actions are no longer functional, adaptive or appropriate. Reinforcement of more appropriate behaviors takes place in normal development; however, neurosis and other forms of pathology can also develop. Changing these behaviors requires identification of the behaviors or symptoms initially. Then modification takes place. One form of behavior modification is called systematic desensitization and is used to treat anxiety disorders. According to behavior modification theory, anxiety is a learned response to environmental stimuli or "triggers." Systematic desensitization helps the individual overcome pathological anxiety by approaching the feared object gradually in an emotional state which inhibits anxiety. Relaxation training is utilized. A hierarchy of anxiety producing objects is developed also with the low intensity objects of stimulation approached initially. Another approach is flooding where the individual is presented with increasing or graded objects of anxiety in a safe clinical setting.

Positive reinforcement of desired behaviors as well as negative reinforcement of unwanted behaviors is the basis of behavior modification. Changing behavior is a complex task requiring a skilled therapist; however, in conjunction with therapy, family members can reinforce positive behaviors. The purpose of effective parenting training is to teach parents to develop these skills.

Hypnosis is another form of therapy. Hypnosis is simply concentration with diminished peripheral awareness. With training this concentration can be self-induced. Hypnosis has been used to decrease anxiety, manage pain and gain insight into repressed thoughts, and to treat addictions, as well as change unwanted habits and behaviors such as smoking and overeating. Biofeedback is related to hypnosis in that physiological functions such as heart beat can be controlled by the individual.

We have discussed some of the treatment approaches used by the therapist. These approaches can be utilized in conjunction with psychotropic medication as well as in various settings. Therapy usually takes place on an outpatient basis; however, in some cases of extreme risk such as the possibility of harm to self or others or severe decompensation, psychiatric hospitalization might be necessary. Recently, less intensive treatment environments are being utilized to treat mental illness. This was initially related to cost considerations; studies suggest that intensive outpatient therapy is, in many cases, not only cost effective but also effective therapeutically.

Many inpatient facilities are developing day care treatment programs. Intensive day care programs are especially useful where there is the need to remove the individual from a detrimental or harmful environment, or where behaviors must be monitored. Examples are adolescent eating disorder situations where intake of food can be controlled and monitored, and the treatment of drug addictions where supply can be prevented. Intensive outpatient treatment programs have the benefit of providing focused, and specific therapy. Various approaches can be used. A program including individual, group and family therapy is often developed. The benefit of the more intensive treatment programs is that behaviors can be monitored and often changes made which might take much longer in less intensive therapy.

Outpatient therapy is the most common type of therapy. Usually the individual participates in therapy once a week. Insurance often covers part of the expense of therapy. Strangely, coverage is often better for inpatient treatment than outpatient care. As the cost benefits of intensive outpatient care and preventative care become more evident, it is hoped that mental health coverage will compensate the programs and providers who prove that they can provide care in the least intensive setting.

Basically there are three types of therapy — individual, group and family therapy. Individual psychotherapy is one on one therapy. Anyone of the therapeutic approaches mentioned can be utilized in one to one therapy. In the process, problems are identified and problem solving techniques developed. Individuals gain insight through introspection and self-analysis. Repressed emotions are explored and relationship styles and issues examined. Better methods of dealing with stress and anxiety are developed. Individuals become more functional and and develop adaptive behaviors and identify goals and directions in their lives. Individual therapy is useful not only in dealing with dysfunctional attitudes and behaviors but in growing and developing a sense of serenity and identity.

There are two types of groups which are considered therapeutic. One type is the self-help group in which there is no trained leader or facilitator. The other is the therapeutic group led by a trained professional.

The best known self-help group is Alcoholics Anonymous (AA). Other groups in operation today include Alanon, which is a group for family members of those who are chemically dependent. There are also groups for incest victims, abused spouses, individuals who are dependent on cocaine (Cocaine Anonymous) and Narcotics Anonymous for those dependent on a variety of mood altering drugs. Overeaters Anonymous is for those with eating problems. The National Association for the Mentally Ill is a powerful organization dedicated to helping individuals with mental illnesses and for family members. All of these groups are voluntary groups with the members remaining anonymous. They are beneficial in that they provide support as well as education. Individuals with addictions and other problems realize that they are not alone and that there is hope.

These self-help groups use what is called a "12 Step Program." There are 12 steps to recovery as well as 12 "tasks." It is significant that the steps are similar to the developmental stages in Erik Erikson's model of psychosocial development. In effect, "Working the steps" is a form of development and provides growth. These steps allow one to advance socially as well as emotionally. The first steps in AA are related to the development of Trust. The next have to do with self-responsibility which is parallel to Erikson's concept of Industry and Initiative. The AA steps involving a personal inventory relate to Erikson's stage of Identity. Making amends is necessary for Intimacy. The last two stages focus on helping others in their recovery, which is comparable to Erikson's Generativity and Ego Integrity stages. Sponsorship is a form of generativity and helping others as a teacher and role model.

The AA mottos provide inspiration and guidelines for a happy, healthy, successful life for those in recovery as well as others. They include, "One Day at a Time," "Take It Easy" and "Let Go, Let God." "God" is considered to be a higher power rather than a religious concept.

Professional therapists have used group therapy for a number of years. One of the most prevalent uses of group therapy is to improve reality testing and overcome denial of problems, especially in cases of chemical dependency. Individuals in recovery, as well as those still actively addicted, are able to share their experiences and problems and how they approach the future. Adolescents who are chemically dependent or are having behavioral problems tend to reject adult authority and resist change. Peer confrontation in group therapy is an effective way of overcoming denial.

Group therapy is often used to improve interpersonal skills and socialization. Group therapy has been used in the treatment of schizophrenia, mood disorders, and anxiety disorders. Group therapy is often used concurrently with individual and family therapy, especially in intensive treatment programs, both outpatient and inpatient.

Group psychotherapy differs from self-help groups in that a trained facilitator is involved. The facilitator or group leader is usually either a social worker, certified addictions counselor, or psychologist. Groups run from one hour to three hours. Some of the groups are structured with specific goals such as improving social skills or the alleviation of depression. Other groups are more spontaneous and allow for the group to decide the direction and focus. Groups are very helpful in ventilating repressed feelings as well as developing problem solving skills. In all cases, the goal is to produce healthy and adaptive change.

Family therapy, which includes marital therapy, is used in various settings and situations. It is often used in conjunction with other forms of therapy, especially when one of the family members is suffering from a severe mental illness. The involvement of a trained clinician is beneficial in that there is direction to the therapy and order in developing coping mechanisms and bringing about change. This does not mean that the family member cannot take the initiative and utilize the techniques outlined in this book; only that in some cases family therapy is more effective and efficient.

There are various models of family therapy. We have discussed briefly the "systems" approach. In family systems therapy the therapist must enter the family system. He or she becomes the change agent, pointing out patholog cal rules and interpersonal relationships and helps the family make changes. Expectations and needs are discussed and negotiated. Communication patterns are explored and suggestions made.

Family therapy can be a growth process as can individual and group therapy. It is probable that in the future psychotherapy will be utilized more fully in helping those with mental illnesses as well as others gain personal insight, identify their emotions and needs, develop their skills and abilities, and lead more functional, rich and fulfilled lives.

Chapter XXXI

LOCATING PROFESSIONAL HELP

Once the decision is made to seek outside help for mental illness in the family, there are a number of complications. Finding competent, trained, experienced professional help is not always easy. The treatment of mental illness is a complicated process. Therapy is more than just "talking" about one's problems. It is probable that a number of pathological attitudes and behaviors have developed over time. Functional disabilities and emotional problems are not solved, necessarily, immediately. Simplistic solutions to complicated and complex problems do not work. Treatment based on inadequate or invalid diagnosis is doomed to failure. Symptoms and pathology may actually become more severe. Thus, it is important, first of all, to locate someone who has the ability to accurately and adequately diagnosis the disorder and the causal factors. For example, the causes of major depression vary. The depression may be primary or secondary. An individual may be depressed because of organic problems or situational life stage factors. The proper treatment depends on the causes and developing a plan to deal with these causes.

Many individuals who present themselves as qualified are not, and in fact, often do not have the education, certification, background and experience to treat emotional problems and mental illnesses. Unqualified individuals can call themselves "therapist" and "counselor." These terms are not regulated by law in most states, and individuals using these titles are not necessarily qualified.

States do, on the other hand, regulate the use of the titles for social worker, physician, addiction counselor and psychologist by certification or licensure. Licensure delineates the procedures which can be performed by the practitioner. Registration refers to the title used. For example, the word, "psychologist" and use of this title is regulated and controlled by law. Thus, a person is called a "registered psychologist." However, most states have become more specific in regulation and identify procedures for each profession. As an example, a medical doctor can prescribe medications. (In some states psychologists with special training

171

can also prescribe psychotropic medication. This trend is becoming more prevalent because psychologists are usually more involved in treatment and thus possibly more able to monitor side effects and responses to psychotropic medication than the general practitioner or family physician.) Licensed psychologists are able to provide psychological and neuropsychological assessment by law in most states, whereas, social workers specialize in other areas.

Initially, social workers began as specialists in providing social services to families and individuals. Their area of expertise was working with clients and helping them develop community support systems and utilize community services. More recently social workers have entered the field of psychotherapy. They provide social assessments and histories, help linkage with community services, focus on aftercare and, in some cases, lead groups and provide individual psychotherapy. Most states license social workers. A Master's Degree in Social Work (MSW) normally requires an undergraduate degree and two years of graduate training.

Medical doctors are trained to treat physical illnesses. While the general practitioner is licensed to prescribe medication including anti-anxiety medications and other psychotropic drugs, they normally do not do psychological evaluations or have extensive training in treating mental illnesses or chemical dependency. A psychiatrist, after four years of training as a generalist, receives three to four years of training as a mental health professional.

After receiving a bachelor's degree, psychologists spend an average of seven additional years in training before receiving a doctorate. Core knowledge areas include biological bases of behavior including neuro-psychology and psychopharmachology; cognitive-affective basis of behavior which covers learning, memory, thinking and emotion; social basis of behavior which covers social psychological, group processes and systems therapy; and individual basis of behavior including personality theory, human development and abnormal psychology. One year of post doctorate and one year of predoctorate internship is usually required prior to taking a state board licensing examination. Psychologists specialize in psychotherapy, and psychological and neuropsychological assessment. Normally an assessment takes from three to five hours and includes the evaluation of intellectual, emotional and functional abilities. Recently psychologists have developed assessment batteries to test for Attention Deficit Disorder and Alzheimer's disease.

In the last ten years a specialty has developed in the treatment of chemical dependency. State, as well as national, certification based on training, education and experience has been developed. Specialists are identified as Certified Addiction Counselors (CAC's). Various levels of certification are available. Mental health specialists, such as psychologists and social workers often become certified as addiction counselors. This is beneficial in that chemical abuse and dependency is often a primary or secondary problem in dysfunctional families and in psychopathology.

Choosing a therapist or getting professional help is complicated by the fact that there are many well meaning "counselors" or "therapists" who are not trained or qualified. It is also complicated by the various professionals and different treatment approaches.

There are a number of questions which should be answered when seeking professional help. Do not hesitate to be assertive and ask these questions. One question which should be asked is the level of training and education as well as whether or not the individual is certified or licensed.

A second question should be the treatment approach. Questions such as the method of diagnosis, the projected time for treatment, family involvement, and costs should be answered.

Questions regarding professional memberships and continuing education are important as well as staff affiliations in situations where hospitalization might be required. Some clinics offer the services of various mental health professionals. This might be of benefit. In many cases psychologists have an association with a physician who can prescribe psychotropic medication. Physicians, conversely, probably should have an affiliation with a professional who is trained in psychotherapy.

Referral sources include local, county and state mental health associations and centers, psychiatric hospitalizations, state and national associations such as the American Psychiatric Association and the American Psychological Association. Often school counselors and the clergy can make recommendations. Individuals who have been in treatment can also provide information. Self-help groups are listed in the phone book. Professionals are also listed. Choosing the appropriate professional can be facilitated by asking the questions listed above.

Conclusion. This book is dedicated to those who have had or are experiencing emotional problems and mental illness and to their family members, in the hope that what has been presented has been helpful and educational. The purpose of the book is to help you and your family understand the symptoms of mental illness and to realize that mental illness should not cause shame or guilt for the individual suffering from the disorder. Once the symptoms are recognized, there is help. Treatment advances in the last decade, in the areas of psychopharmacology and psychotherapy, have allowed millions of individuals suffering from mental illness to lead healthy, happy, complete lives. May you and your family benefit from what you have learned in this book and begin to make healthy and adaptive changes not only in your view of mental illness but in the ways you cope with the related problems.

INDEX

Date Due